the best
KIND OF DIFFERENT

the best
KIND OF DIFFERENT

Our Family's Journey with Asperger's Syndrome

SHONDA SCHILLING

With an Introduction by Curt Schilling
and a
Foreword by Peter B. Rosenberger, M.D., founder of the
Learning Disorders Unit, Massachusetts General Hospital

WILLIAM MORROW
An Imprint of HarperCollinsPublishers

All photographs are courtesy of the author unless otherwise noted.

The medical information in this book is given for informational purposes only and should not be considered a substitute for the advice of the reader's physician or other health care professional. Certain names have been changed throughout to protect the privacy of minors and others discussed in this book.

HarperCollins books may be purchased for educational, business, or sales promotional use. For information please write: Special Markets Department, HarperCollins Publishers, 10 East 53rd Street, New York, NY 10022.

FIRST EDITION

Library of Congress Cataloging-in-Publication Data has been applied for.

ISBN 978-0-06-198683-3

10 11 12 13 14   OV/RRD   10 9 8 7 6 5 4 3 2 1

This book is dedicated to my family and friends, without whom this journey would have never been possible. Your love and support has sustained me and driven me to be a better mother, wife, and friend.

And to Grant, whose endless love makes every day a new adventure.

Contents

Foreword
PETER B. ROSENBERGER, M.D.

※

SHONDA AND CURT SCHILLING FIRST BROUGHT THEIR SON
Grant to see me the summer of 2007. At that time, he was about to be in second
grade and at seven-and-a-half-years old, he was having problems with behavior
and classroom function. For a number of reasons, it seemed that attention deficit was playing a role in his behavior; however, on my first encounter with
Grant it was clear that something else was involved—a basic problem with
social interaction. It was then that I raised the likelihood that Grant's struggles
were the result of Asperger syndrome.

The Schillings are justifiably proud of their children, and initially this was
a bitter pill for them to swallow. Their response was first to provide Grant
with the best intervention available, and second to learn everything they could
about the disorder. The result is that two-and-a-half years later, Grant and his
family are managing as well as any family I have had with this diagnosis.

So, what is this disorder? In 1944 Hans Asperger, an Austrian pediatrician
with a special interest in exceptional children, published a report in a German
psychiatric journal under the title "The 'Autistic Psychopathies' of Child-

hood." While Asperger himself achieved prominence in academic medicine after the war, the report languished in obscurity, and was not even translated into English until 1991.

The four cases described in considerable detail by Asperger in the original report formed the core of what is now known as Asperger syndrome. As soon as the report came to light, readers recognized the remarkable similarities between Asperger's children and those described in 1943 by Leo Kanner, the Austrian psychiatrist who was the first to describe infantile autism. Although Kanner and Asperger never met, both had borrowed the term *autistic*, coined decades earlier by the Swiss psychiatrist Eugen Bleuler, to describe a peculiar type of thinking, driven primarily not by perceptions but by feelings. Both Kanner and Asperger observed in their children a fundamental incapacity for social interaction, along with restricted repertoires of behavior, fixations of interest on certain objects or subjects, abnormalities of language, and atypical responses to sensory input of all kinds.

While the similarities between the two groups are obvious, the differences are just as striking. The Asperger children tend to be of average intelligence and have better language skills than Kanner's autists, many of whom are mute. Though both groups share an inability to conceive of what is going on in another person's mind, in the Asperger cases, this deficit can be limited, requiring more sophisticated tests to identify it. In addition, an Asperger child may be relatively comfortable with physical expressions of affection, although most autistic children struggle with this. Strikingly preserved abilities (savant skills) exist in both groups, but they are more dramatically demonstrated by the Asperger children. Both syndromes are more likely in boys than girls, but this gender difference is more pronounced for the Asperger group. While the Asperger person may be socially clumsy, he is less likely than the Kanner autist to be totally oblivious of the humanity of other people in the room, treating them like pieces of the furniture.

These clinical differences between Asperger syndrome and autism have inevitably raised the issue of whether the two are different disorders, or whether the one is merely a milder form of the other. The controversy persists, although the conventional wisdom today is that the autistic disorders occur along a spectrum, of both type and severity. *Autism spectrum disorder* is in fact currently the favored term among many prominent clinicians, and will probably appear as such in the next edition of the *Diagnostic and Statistical Manual of Mental Disorder*s published by the American Psychiatric Association.

On the whole, autistic thinking displays a lack of awareness of what another person is feeling. This is best tested in kids by posing situations in which the thoughts of another person are contrary to fact. The classic example goes likes this: Sally has a basket; Annie has a box. Sally has a ball in her basket. Sally leaves the room, and while she is away, naughty Annie takes the ball from Sally's basket and hides it in her own box. Sally returns to the room. She wants to play with her ball. Where does she look for it? A normal child will respond, "In the basket." Why? "Because that's where she thinks it is." A child with autistic spectrum disorder will answer, "In the box." Why? "Because that's where it is, silly."

In people with Asperger syndrome, this type of thinking can stand out in stark contrast to their otherwise highly developed abilities. Popular understanding of Asperger syndrome has been greatly enhanced by the comic strip *Dilbert*, which deals with a highly intelligent engineer trying to cope with corporate idiocy. Dilbert's superiors, from the CEO down to his pointy-haired department manager, are indeed numbskulls. However, Dilbert expresses his frustrations so maladroitly that he insults his bosses, alienates customers, and torpedoes all prospective romantic relationships on the first date. In so doing he makes clear to us that whether a particular stance is moderate or extreme depends upon your point of view. One person's frankness is another person's rudeness, and that person's tact is yet another person's hypocrisy.

Similarly, children on the autism spectrum can have prodigious reading mechanics and spelling skills, yet not the slightest clue of the message intended by the sentence or paragraph, particularly if it is a social one. On standard intelligence tests, they do relatively well on measures of rote information, immediate memory, and block design, but poorly on social comprehension ("What do you do if you find a stamped letter lying on the street?") or arranging pictures in sequence to tell a story. Then there are the savant skills that some display. Though not all can do it, a common skill for Asperger children is to tell the day of the week on which a particular calendar date will occur, for as much as a hundred years in the past or future. I once had a teenage patient who could tell me the product of any pair of two- or three-digit numbers instantly upon hearing the numbers spoken. Another patient, nine years old, could tell me the make of any automobile, domestic or foreign, from a picture of the taillight. It is still not clear whether such skills occur because the child's brain is different, or simply because he obsessively pours all of his cognitive effort into a limited number or skills.

Atypical responses to the outside world are another feature of all autistic syndromes. The same child who responds to your voice as if he were stone deaf will hold his ears in fright when the fire truck goes down the street three blocks away. They can also show revulsion for other sensory stimuli, such as the texture of certain foods, wool socks, or the labels on shirt collars. This response is termed *sensory defensiveness* by occupational therapists, and is occasionally seen in the absence of any other autistic features. On the other hand, some more severely autistic children who recoil from affectionate personal contact will enjoy rough handling and horseplay.

Given the variety of ways in which the syndrome shows itself, parenting a child with Asperger syndrome poses a unique and trying set of challenges. For one thing, many common parenting instincts frequently have to be reined in—most notably the desire to hug and show physical affection with the child. Because of their sensitivity to touch, many Asperger children struggle with being hugged by their parents. Their verbal behavior can often appear rude or dismissive, but again this is largely rooted in the fact that they don't process language in the same way that you or I do.

The most fortunate Asperger children are those with parents who are committed to helping the child cope with and overcome limitations in language pragmatics and social comprehension. As one parent of an autistic teenager once told me, "You can get over failing a course or two in high school, but you can't get over never being invited to the prom."

Regular pediatric visits with the child and family to help everyone cope can be invaluable. The doctor should also be able to cut through the noise and give you sound medical advice. Given the proliferation of websites, magazine articles, and books, it can be hard to distill the information into that which is most relevant, and the doctor should be able to help.

One of the most helpful insights for a family can be understanding how a child with Asperger syndrome is limited in his or her comprehension of language. While atypical responses from Asperger kids can be frustrating, they are easier for a parent to tolerate when he or she understands that Asperger kids really don't interpret language in the same way. Though many parents insist that their child understands every word they say, with children on the autism spectrum this is frequently not the case, especially when the message is social in nature. This can be hard for some parents to accept, but once they do, the end result is less frustration all around.

Medications can be helpful, but they must be used with care. Medications to improve social awareness have been tried, with some limited success. Many, perhaps most, children across the autism spectrum have attention deficits, yet such deficits don't always respond to stimulant medications. Still they are definitely worth a try if the attention deficit impacts on cognitive function. (Grant and his teachers find stimulant medication quite helpful for his classroom performance and adjustment.)

Because Asperger children tend to be higher functioning, they can usually benefit from classroom instruction alongside their peers. However, it's important to talk to their school about options for helping the child cope. While Asperger kids can thrive in a normal classroom setting, it is especially important that they have teachers who can help them deal with the maladaptive behaviors that jeopardize their adjustment to the group.

It's been two and a half years now, and I can safely say that Grant is doing very well. I've seen a marked improvement as both he and his parents have adjusted to the diagnosis. He is able to function better at school and participate in more successful ways; and to hear his parents tell it, a lot less yelling goes on now.

While things have improved, Asperger syndrome is something the family must deal with on a daily basis, and the campaign to help Grant adjust is a constant challenge for his family and teachers. It's my hope that the chronicle that follows will inspire other families and caregivers to accept this challenge and help Asperger children adjust to what frequently appears to them a hostile world. The book you are about to read is special, but the story is one that plays out everyday, as parents everywhere must confront the same diagnosis with which Curt, Shonda, and Grant have been dealing. Only an understanding of the condition on the human level will enable what Curt and Shonda have accomplished—to turn the cold clinical word *atypical* into *the best kind of different*.

the best
KIND OF DIFFERENT

Introduction

✳

"I NEED TO TALK TO YOU."

For any husband, those six words are usually accompanied by the head tilt or eye roll, because they're usually followed by a conversation pointing out that you've done or said something terribly wrong. In 2007, when I heard those words in a Chicago hotel room, I thought that was where I was headed. I quickly realized that was not the case. Shonda sat down on the bed, eyes watering, and uttered five words I'll remember until the day I die:

"Grant has autism spectrum disorder."

I've experienced some serious highs and lows in my lifetime—losing my father suddenly in front of my eyes to an aortic aneurism, winning three World Series championships, being told my wife has cancer. This new piece of information hit me with the same level of impact. Inwardly I am a very emotional, very passionate person, which can be both a good and a bad thing. However, in times of crisis, I know how to keep it together. This was such a time. I didn't overreact, I didn't cry or go nuts. I said, "Okay, now what?" Or words to that effect. I don't know any other way to handle situations like that, other than to immediately accept where you are, figure out where to go, and get moving.

That said, and having attention-deficit/hyperactivity disorder (ADHD) myself, it wasn't long before my mind started racing. On the first lap I nearly crashed and burned as countless visions from eight years of chastising, punishing, yelling, and some spanking popped into my head. I was overcome with an immediate and overwhelming sense of guilt, horrible painful guilt only the parent of a child he loves more than life itself could possibly know. At the same time, about ten different pieces of the undecipherable puzzle that was Grant fell into place. I didn't know what ASD meant specifically, but I knew that answers were coming—answers we'd thought we were years to a lifetime from having were now right on the horizon.

All our children are unique in their own ways, but Grant is *very* unique. Grant did things that befuddled me, which in and of itself isn't odd for an eight-year-old. But the degree to which Grant marched to his own drummer seemed very unusual. Most remarkably, the depth of emotion Grant felt and expressed went far beyond what I'd witnessed in many adults. Sometimes I was proud that a kid could love so deeply so young. Other times I was insanely upset that a kid could be standing in front of me, looking in my general direction, hear a specific set of orders, turn around, and not act on a single one of those orders. It was maddening, it was stupefying, and, at the very least, it was incredibly confusing.

For a long time, Grant was an issue between Shonda and me. My job playing baseball for the Boston Red Sox required me to travel a lot. I was on the road for literally nine months a year. Toward the end of my career I saw more of my wife and kids when they went on a road trip with me than when I was at home. While traveling with the team, my "parenting" was done courtesy of AT&T. Congratulations, good nights, happy birthdays, admonishments, punishments, and many other parental duties were carried out over fiber-optic telephone lines. As my career started to wind down, Shonda and I talked less and less over the phone. Too often she'd call totally exhausted from a day with our kids, upset as well, and tell me, "When you get home you need to punish Gehrig, scold Grant, tell Gabby she cannot do that, and tell Garrison he has to do X." My response was often, "No, I can't, I won't. I am not going to be away for ten days, talking to my kids for a total of fifteen minutes, and then walk through the door and start spanking them. It's not going to happen."

This usually resulted in either a heated argument or a really short phone call. Both of us had been pushed to the ends of our ropes, and neither of us wanted to admit our shortcomings as parents. These unpleasant conversations had the detrimental effect of making us want to avoid talking. She called less often, we talked less, and we really "communicated" barely at all. With arguments creeping into every conversation we had, I think we both assumed that if we didn't talk, we couldn't argue. I was dealing with a ton of issues in my day job, and Red Sox Nation is not a patient bunch. It's win or go home. But looking back, that isn't and cannot be a valid excuse for any of my actions or reactions.

As much as it pains me to say this, the fact is that for much of my baseball career, our home felt essentially like a single-parent home. I knew no other way to do what I did for a living than to immerse myself in the game of baseball 24/7, 365 days a year. I was the provider for our family, and in my mind, working hard to be the best in the world at what I did was the same thing as being a devoted dad. While I was certainly never the best, I never stopped wanting or striving for that. I can remember one day in Arizona, sitting at a red light with Grant in the car. He was asking me about Pokémon cards. He kept asking, and I was in my own deep thought, until he finally yelled, *"Dad! Why aren't you listening to me?"* I was thinking about how I wanted to change my approach to pitching to Paul Lo Duca next time I faced him. It was December 28, and spring training was still three months away.

The thing about Asperger's is that it's tough to phone in. To really understand it you have to be face-to-face with it every day. You have to wake up with it, eat breakfast with it, take it to school, and try as hard as you can to get it to go to soccer practice (Asperger's apparently really, *really* hates wearing shin guards). Shonda knew—even before the diagnosis—that something was not right. Grant was different, and by different she meant *different*. She's rarely been wrong, but when it comes to the kids she's never been wrong. While I had my suspicions, what I suspected was nothing out of the ordinary, nothing that more parenting and more discipline wouldn't fix. Now that I'm there every day, I can see just how wrong I was.

Over the past three years, my wife and I have experienced a lifetime of growth. We've brought our marriage to a place one dreams of being but few achieve. People have often asked me in the past two years since I stopped playing baseball, "Don't you miss it?" My response has been a very quick and very adamant, "I miss absolutely nothing about the game of baseball, nothing."

That response is a direct result of our kids and, I would argue, mainly Grant and the education he's providing us with on a daily basis. Grant's situation has forced Shonda and me to look at ourselves in plain daylight, no filters, to assess who we are and what we are as parents. I know I didn't even remotely like what I saw upon first glance, and since then I've worked hard to make noticeable changes, changes I am still working on to this day.

Looking back, and having helped her through this book, I had no idea she'd gone through some of the things she has, just like she has no idea of some of the things I endured over the past five years. But I don't think either one of us has or will allow that to affect where we are today, and where our family is. She's managed to raise four children who love unconditionally (albeit four children who can still raise the hair on your neck at a moment's notice). She's managed to undergo a massive transformation as a mother, a wife, and woman that very few women her age would even consider, and she's done it for our children, and our marriage.

I can't imagine one day of the past twenty years of my life not having this wonderful world-changing woman in it, and I pray I never have to. The book you hold tells of a journey neither of us wanted to go on, yet the Lord knew we could do it, that we could survive it, and that she could help others by sharing it. For that I am eternally grateful and proud to call her my wife.

CURT SCHILLING
December 22, 2009

one
Our Less-Than-Perfect Family Moment

✳

TO THOSE WHO KNOW MY SON GRANT AND ME, I FREQUENTLY referred to it as the summer that one or both of us would end up medicated.

It was 2007, and Grant was seven. I was rounding the bend toward forty, but there were moments when I was so worn out I felt more like seventy. Every day was filled with exhausting challenges, one after another.

On a visit to my hometown of Baltimore, Maryland, that summer, I somehow got it in my head that I should take Grant along with my other kids—Gehrig, then twelve, Gabby, ten, and Garrison, four—to an Orioles baseball game. I suppose it was wishful thinking on my part. There were so many reasons it could have been a special evening—so many reasons to be sentimental. Not only had I grown up going to Orioles games at the old Memorial Stadium, taking in game after game there with my dad, mom, and brother, mostly in the one-dollar bleachers, but the Orioles were also how I met my husband, Curt, who used to pitch for them.

To make that particular game in the summer of 2007 even more exciting, Curt was pitching again, only this time for the opposing team, the Boston

Red Sox. I wanted the kids to be there for that—to see "our" team play my home team.

When we got to the stadium, I proudly led the kids up to the stands. Then . . .

"I wanna go!"

Grant was visibly upset, his face a bright red.

"I wanna go! I wanna go!" he started chanting over and over while holding his hands over his ears. He draped his upper body over my knees and started rolling back and forth aggressively as he screamed.

Luckily it was loud in the stadium. People were milling about, shouting at one another, and cheering. There were announcements and music over the PA. But it wasn't so loud that Grant's tantrum went unnoticed. All nearby heads turned in our direction. People had the most concerned looks on their faces, as if to say, "What did you do to your kid, lady?" A few more I-wanna-gos and the expression morphed into an indignant "Jeez, why can't you get control of your kid?"

And then they opened their mouths.

"Grant!" one of the men shouted. *"You need to listen to your mom!"*

"Calm down, Grant!" one of the women said.

Have you ever heard the expression "If you want to help, don't"? It's a good one. Those people meant well, but they were only making matters worse, not to mention making me feel even more humiliated.

Despite entertaining vivid thoughts of killing those people (or perhaps just seriously injuring them), I managed to smile through gritted teeth. I needed to put on a good face. People might recognize me, and they were clearly judging me, assuming I didn't know how to control my kid. They weren't too far off base, but I didn't need them to point that out to everyone around us. Plus, it just made Grant more upset.

"Grant, we need to stay here," I said as firmly and quietly as I could, still all smiles. Grant didn't stop, though.

"*I wanna go, nooooow!*" he shouted again. He continued flailing, and I worried that he might hit himself on the aluminum chair in front of him. I tried to hold him, but he wouldn't have it.

Then I tried bribing him. "We'll go to the toy store tomorrow, Grant," I offered.

Nothing.

"You can pick the movie tonight."

"You can stay in my bed."

"You can have cotton candy. We can have popcorn."

Still nothing.

Frankly, at that point, I would have let him eat a hot dog with cotton candy for a bun and ice cream on top just to get him to stop. But none of my offers worked. (Of course, the next day he would still remember I'd promised a trip to the toy store, and he'd insist on it.)

"Let me take him for a walk," my mom offered. I felt bad. I didn't want her to miss this game, either. "Grant, come for a walk," she said, reaching for his hand, but he kept rocking and screaming. He only wanted me. But there was nothing I could do to make him happy.

I felt completely defeated. I wanted nothing more than for Grant to *want* to be there. But not only did he not want to be there, he didn't even understand what was going on. For a long time I had been trying, unsuccessfully, to get Grant excited about baseball. I wanted him to be able to bond with his dad the way his siblings had, but in his seven years, that hadn't really happened. There was a disconnect that I couldn't understand, and nothing I tried seemed to fix it.

At the game, I couldn't even get Grant to grasp that it was his father down there on the field, that he was one of the greatest pitchers in baseball, playing right there in this game that had brought all these fans to this huge stadium. I just kept thinking, *If Grant sees Curt out there, he will take an interest. He will understand it, and he will be proud.* I thought about how many kids would give anything to be sitting in those stands, let alone watching their father pitch for the Red Sox. What would it take to get Grant to realize what this all meant?

However, Grant wanted nothing to do with being in the stands. Once the game started, I tried to calm him down by showing him how to mark the scorecard and keep track of every play. But he was agitated and couldn't focus. I found myself caught between a rock and a hard place: It seemed as if I should get us all out of there before Grant made a bigger scene, but that wouldn't be fair to Gehrig, Gabby, and Garrison. I didn't want any of us to miss that game, because I knew that Curt's career was coming to an end. Also, the kids had begun to have their own lives. A family vacation was going to become difficult to pull together with any regularity now that the kids had obligations to sports and camp and other things they wanted to do with their friends. I didn't know how many more moments like this we were going to get, and I wanted us all to have a memory of this special night before it was gone.

My heart sank and I started to wonder if the seat I was sitting on would be big enough for me to fit underneath. I wanted to find a place to hide. How much more of Grant's screaming could we all take? Fortunately, he started running out of steam. He climbed into my lap and began rocking back and forth, back and forth, covering his ears, without saying a word. This was hardly an ideal way for me to watch the game. But it was preferable to fighting with him and listening to him scream.

In a short time, Grant rocked himself to sleep.

———•———

THIS WAS NOT THE first time I'd had a problem with Grant in the stands at a ball game. It had been a long time—years—since I'd tried to take him. I figured he'd be mature enough at seven to behave differently, and maybe even enjoy himself. That's what I thought it was then: a maturity issue.

Since the time Grant was little, I'd known it was better to leave him at the hotel with my mom during away games, or, if it was a home game, put him into our players' kids' room in the stadium. There was a great one in Phoenix that we used when Curt played for the Arizona Diamondbacks from 2000 to 2003. It was staffed with five or six adults who would lead the kids through arts and crafts, video games, and building things with blocks. Grant could get lost in there, playing all day with the other players' kids. It was great for me, too. I needed to have a place where I could put Grant so I could get three hours to myself to enjoy a game.

My experience had been so different with Gehrig and Gabby, and later, with Garrison. Even when they were toddlers, I was able to keep them content at games. I could teach them how to do things like take peanuts out of their shells (that alone would keep them occupied for several innings). But those activities were never enough for Grant. He was never happy at games, and I didn't know why.

If it were just Major League Baseball he had an issue with, maybe it wouldn't have been so bad—even though it would have broken his father's heart, not to mention my own. But the truth is, I couldn't control Grant in most situations. He was noisy, willful, defiant, incapable of sitting still—and that was just the tip of the iceberg.

Later that fateful summer of 2007, it finally clicked for me: Grant was different. Really different. And I realized I needed to do something to help him—to get some kind of professional help, although what that would be, I wasn't yet sure.

I wouldn't come to that realization until I first hit a wall. With a cordless phone, to be very specific. One morning as I tried to get the kids ready and out the door to day camp, I couldn't get Grant going. He wouldn't get up, then he wouldn't brush his teeth, and then he wouldn't get dressed. Everything I asked him to do was met with a resounding *"No!"* Something in me snapped.

I went into his room and yelled at him. He was completely unfazed. I tried grabbing him to put the clothes on his body myself, but he pulled away and ignored me. Here I had just told his little brother, who wasn't even five yet, to get dressed, and he hopped right to it. Why was this seven-year-old so unaffected by what I was asking, so uninterested in listening to an adult? Why couldn't he look me in the eye? I didn't get it, and I wanted to kill him. I knew that if I put my hands on him again, I'd hurt him.

I stormed downstairs loudly, all the while screaming up to Grant, *"You'd better get dressed, young man!"* My kids have rarely seen me flip out—maybe once or twice in their lives. That morning Gehrig, Gabby, and Garrison were shaking in their boots. Grant just stayed in his room, in his pajamas, playing with his Legos as if this conversation never happened. He was obsessed with Legos.

In the kitchen, I grabbed the phone to call Curt, who was on the road. "I want to hurt him!" I sobbed, when Curt answered.

"You're just upset," Curt said.

"No, I mean it. I *really* want to hurt him," I said.

"You just have to show him who's boss, Shonda," Curt suggested. "He needs to respect you."

Curt wasn't getting it. He did not understand that there was something going on here that was not about discipline and respect. I felt so frustrated, I threw the phone against the wall. Then I sat down where the phone had fallen and curled up in the corner, bawling.

I have always believed that being a mother was what I was meant to do, but in that moment I wasn't so sure.

As predicted, it wasn't long before we were both on meds.

two

Motherhood on Baseball Time

✳

TO SOME EXTENT, I ALWAYS KNEW THAT BEING A MOTHER WAS a tough job, even though my mother handled it with incredible grace. What I didn't know was how extra hard motherhood could be when you're married to a professional athlete who is away eight or nine months of the year. I didn't realize that my husband's job would have the power to drastically alter my idyllic vision of being a parent—not to mention confuse things with Grant.

My mother set a great example for me. She relished making childhood fun for my younger brother and me, and always made sure we were well cared for. Even in the hardest of times, there were always three square meals, and you could be sure you were not getting up from that dinner table until you ate all three things on your plate: protein, vegetable, and starch. As I used to tease her, all the colors of the rainbow were represented on our plate.

We had the utmost respect for her, and growing up I always wanted to be just like her. I knew I would get married and have kids of my own, and I imagined that my kids would look up to me and have the same kind of respect for me that I have for my mom. I'd have a fun family, and since I'd been an athlete my whole life, I was certain that sports would play a big part. I just didn't know how *big* a role sports would play. Then I met Curt.

It was 1990, and I was just out of college at Towson State University, where I finished my bachelor's degree after getting an associate's degree at Essex Community College. My first job out of college was as an associate producer at Home Team Sports, which covered all the Baltimore and Washington area sports teams. My love of sports helped me get the job, and it was a perfect fit. I'd grown up going to games and listening to them on the radio. I was a serious fan, but this job gave me a chance to learn more about baseball than I'd ever imagined.

At the time, Curt was playing for the Orioles. He had started his career in 1986, having been drafted by the Boston Red Sox, but in September of 1988 he was traded to the Orioles. At Home Team Sports, I worked the entire baseball season with the Orioles, but only when the team was at home. To compensate for the gaps and make ends meet, I also had a part-time job at a Foot Locker in a nearby mall, where I'd worked throughout college.

While I was there one day in the off-season, Curt walked into the store. We recognized each other from the ballpark and we talked for a few minutes.

"Some friends and I are going out for a drink tomorrow night," he said. "Maybe you and some of your friends would like to meet us?"

I hesitated for a moment. I'd never gone out with a ballplayer, and the close overlap between my work life and my personal life gave me pause. I told him I'd talk to my friends and see if they'd be interested. I ended up going to meet him at the pub, and barely an hour into the evening, everyone else disappeared, leaving Curt and me alone for most of the night. It was the perfect opportunity to get to know each other. We talked all night, and ended up playing Pop-A-Shot, and I beat him. (He claims he let me win, but we all know no true athlete ever lets anyone win.)

At the end of the night, he asked me for my number. I was a little apprehensive, though, because I didn't think it would be a good idea to date him. I had been working only a few months at this exciting job that I'd landed right out of college, and I was afraid that dating him would cost me that job.

"I'll tell you what," I said. "My last name is also the name of a Major League Baseball team. If you really want to find me, look it up." (My maiden name was Brewer.) Sure enough, the next day Curt called my house. He got my cousin, who was also my roommate, on the phone. He knew from our conversation the night before that she loved animals, so he talked her into bringing me to his house to meet his Rottweilers.

"Can I take you to dinner tomorrow night?" he asked, after we'd been at his house awhile.

I said yes, and then called my mom. "A ballplayer asked me out," I casually told her, without offering details.

The next night, October 7, 1990, we had our first date. He took me to an Italian restaurant. I wound up embarrassing myself, ordering food I couldn't recognize. At just twenty-two, having grown up with very modest means, I hadn't been to too many nice restaurants. Curt handled it beautifully. He called the waiter over and helped me order again. He was so kind and sweet, making me feel as if he really wanted to take care of me.

The next day, as my parents were going to work, my mom told my dad, "A young baseball player asked Shonda out."

"I bet it's Curt Schilling," he said. To this day, we still don't know how he knew. His explanation: Curt just seemed like a great person, and a great match for me, personality-wise.

Curt and I quickly became inseparable. The only problem was that I was notified that I was one class short of completing my degree, and since it was the off-season, Curt didn't have anything to do. He kept talking me into playing hooky—taking days off, or just missing a class here and there. We'd spend the time hanging out, eating, watching movies. When Christmas rolled around, we didn't want to be apart. Instead of going to see his family in Colorado, Curt stayed with me and mine.

My dad's instincts about Curt and me were right on. Curt and I were both very much in the same place emotionally—both in our early twenties but done with going out to bars and partying. We'd sown our wild oats and were ready for the next stage in our lives, if it was meant to be. Curt's father had recently passed away, and he was the rock Curt's family was built on, as well as his best friend. As a result, Curt was ready to settle down, and I was beginning to think that perhaps I was, too.

But then a bomb dropped: Just after New Year's in early 1991, Roland Hemond, general manager of the Orioles, called Curt to tell him that the Orioles had made a trade. Specifically, Curt was being traded. To the Houston Astros.

As Curt said the words, I burst into tears. Just when I'd felt comfortable enough to let my guard down and enjoy our relationship, he'd been traded, and to a team halfway across the country. It was my first taste of just how difficult it is to be in love with a baseball player.

Curt saw how upset I was. He looked at me and he said, "You have to go with me." But I couldn't just up and leave everything, including my job, like that. Curt, however, had a plan. "I'll leave for spring training," he said, "and you'll come visit me there. Then we'll move to Houston when the season starts."

The more I thought about it, the more his plan made sense. It didn't take me long to agree to meet him in Houston in April. I spent the next five weeks—while Curt was at spring training—packing, cleaning out the house he'd been renting in Baltimore, hiring a moving truck, and making living arrangements for us. I didn't realize it at the time, but that was my first taste of what being a baseball wife would entail, my first taste of my "job" for the next twenty years or so, always packing and moving and arranging. (At last count, Curt and I had moved over fifty times during his twenty-plus years in the major leagues. For what it's worth, we count moving as any time the house gets packed and the dogs come along for more than a month.)

My mom and I flew out to Houston just a couple of days before the team arrived for its first home series. The first night we had to sleep on the floor— our furniture wouldn't be delivered until the next morning. This was all new to me. Even though I'd had my own apartment, which I shared with my cousin, and I'd done things like arrange to have my utilities hooked up, setting up a house in one weekend was a whole different ball game. I wanted to get it all done for Curt before he came home from that first road trip. I didn't want him to worry about anything but the season.

Opening day was fun, but the home stand wasn't long. Before I knew it, Curt was on the road again. My mom had to go, too. She needed to get back to work. I dropped her off at the airport and then stopped at a Target. That's when it all hit me. At that moment it dawned on me that I had never been farther west than Tennessee in my life. And now here I was in Texas, with no family, no friends, and a whole week before I would see Curt again.

What I didn't realize back then was that as arduous as this move was, it was training for what I'd face later on. In the future, kids would be added to the slew of things that needed to be transitioned from one location to the next—finding new schools, sorting through doctors, saying good-bye to friends. This would be the rhythm of our life together, and it all would occur with varying levels of support from Curt. Sometimes he'd be there to help, but frequently he wouldn't.

———◆———

JUST A COUPLE OF MONTHS into the season, Curt was not doing well as a closer. April had started well, but in May things began to unravel. Before we knew it, he'd been sent down to the minor leagues, and of all places, Tucson, Arizona, even *farther* from my home back east. Once more I found myself in a place I knew nothing about, but after one long month in the minors, Curt went back up to the big leagues.

We were just getting back into the swing of things when my dad came to visit. Little did I know that Curt had asked him for my hand in marriage. It was a hot, humid day (as is every day in Houston) and I was cleaning the house up while Curt kept bothering me to come and see the mail. I would like to say that I was kind and gracious in response to his requests, but I was tired and cranky, and unfortunately we have it all on videotape. When I got to where the pile of mail was on the kitchen table, I sat down and Curt dropped to one knee.

And so, with the season winding down, we got engaged. Curt finished up in middle relief and closing (coming in after the starting pitcher left the game), and my first off-season came as a huge relief. Unfortunately, time moves pretty quickly, and not long after Christmas we packed our dogs and clothes and headed to Orlando for spring training. The six weeks of spring training go fast, too, and before I knew it I was driving the dogs back to Houston with two other wives on the team. Wives usually pack the cars and drive them back from spring training, and this first year I was in a caravan with Patty Biggio and Nancy Caminiti on what would be a two-day drive.

I was listening to the last spring training game of the year on the radio when, about halfway to Houston, I heard, "The big news today: Curt Schilling has just been traded to the Philadelphia Phillies." I was almost an accident statistic before I had a chance to be a bride; I could barely keep my car on the road.

When I got hold of Curt, we only had a few minutes to talk. He was taking off to meet the Philadelphia team in Miami on the final day of spring training. I would continue the ten-hour journey to Houston, pack the house up, get the first flight out of there, and once again find us a place to live in a new city. I wouldn't even get a chance to say good-bye to anyone.

As hard as it was to fathom relocating yet again, I was very happy about this move, in part because it would put me back on the East Coast, not too far from my parents. I've always hated being far from my family, and this was almost like being traded back home.

———·———

IT'S AMAZING HOW ONE decision by one person can change everything in your world. While Curt was throwing in the Phillies bullpen the very next day, in a downpour of rain, his new pitching coach, Johnny Podres, took notice. "You throw way too hard to be a closer," the coach said. "You've got a Hall of Fame arm, kid. We're going to make you a starter someday!"

Those two sentences changed our lives forever. Curt really began to shine. He was on his way to becoming one of the greatest starters in baseball, all because one guy decided to give him that chance.

The 1992 season was a successful one, and the following November, we got married. The ceremony was in the church I'd started going to when I was in the second grade, just down the block from my parents' home in Dundalk, Maryland. In the beginning, I'd gone because a friend of mine went. My family didn't do church. Ever. I suppose I was searching for something, some kind of deeper meaning to life.

Without fail, I went every Sunday. When I was very young, my mom would walk me across the street and right to the door, and she would be waiting for me when I got out. When I got a little older, I went on my own. I went all the way through to confirmation. There was this really devout wonderful older congregant who watched over all the kids. I called him Uncle Tommy from the day I met him, until the day he died in the late 1990s. He was a lifelong friend and someone I can't imagine having lived without.

"Will you be my acolyte?" he'd ask again and again.

"Okay," I'd say, and there was something about it that made me feel accountable in a good way.

Church and spirituality have been big parts of my life ever since. One of the beliefs instilled in me in church was that it is important to do for others. When you do something for someone in need, the feeling you get is infinitely better than anything else life has to offer.

In 1993 I was happy to have the opportunity to begin helping others. That's when Curt and I were introduced to Dick Bergeron, a patient with amyotrophic lateral sclerosis (ALS), also known as Lou Gehrig's disease. ALS is a cruel disease in which patients progressively lose muscle function—and their dignity—while their minds remain intact. We were both so affected by his story and his struggle, we desperately wanted to do something. A great woman named Ellyn Phillips, president of the ALS Association, offered us the opportunity to spread the word as spokespeople, an offer we happily accepted.

That was also the year Curt began to establish his reputation as a "big game pitcher." I have so many memories of that year, on and off the field— going to the playoffs, watching my husband break a National League Championship Series record by striking out the first five batters of the game, hearing my heart pound like a hammer, all because of this energy he created.

Ironically, I almost didn't get to see some of the most exciting moments. The wives weren't officially allowed on the road, in hotel bars, or anywhere that might be considered the players' space. The team leaders of that early 1990s Phillies team were a self-described "Macho Row," who stayed out late after games and, in my opinion, showed no respect for their wives. If a young player like Curt didn't do what they did, he'd find himself the target of their immature behavior. (I could write a book about those guys alone. All I can say is that karma is a tough thing, and in the end, they all got what they deserved.)

Curt didn't want any part of that, and he had a saving grace: He could handle their making fun of him, because the bottom line was that they wanted him to have the ball in their most important games. There was a game in Pittsburgh—the final game, when Philly would clinch the National League East pennant. One of the veteran wives said to us younger women, "You get in your car and go."

"But we're not allowed," I said.

"Well, I'm going and so are some others," she insisted. "You don't know if you'll ever get this close to a World Series again. You want to see this!"

She had a point. To sit through all those home games and then not be allowed to watch the most important moments in person? Not be allowed to celebrate? Sure enough, I got in my car and I went. We won the National League East that night. We were going to the playoffs. It would be eight years before we went to another postseason, so I'm especially glad I went.

I say "we" went to the World Series because when you're married to a baseball player, it's as if you've both been hired by the team. It's kind of like when a couple says, "We're pregnant," when it's obvious who's carrying that baby. It still belongs to both of them, the same way the baseball life belonged to both of us. Often I'll say that "we" were traded, or that "we" were on this team or that team. That's what you say when you're a baseball wife. As a wife you may not be on the payroll, but you're the one who takes care of everything in life that your husband can't do—be it packing or parenting. Very few professional athletes' marriages work any differently.

In Philly, it wasn't easy being a rookie wife. It was a very veteran team, with players who'd been there a long time. Back then, that was more common on many teams. The wives were no different. In the same way the rookie players had to earn their way up the ladder, the wives did as well, and often there was more hostility in the stands than in the clubhouse. That's one of the hardest things about being a baseball wife. You find yourself in new cities, whether just for a short while or for a few years, and you know no one. As if that's not hard enough, the other wives are reluctant to bond too strongly with new women—especially women who are just the players' girlfriends—because you never know when your men will get traded. And you also never know when the women will get traded for younger models. It's very hard to get close to a woman and become really good friends and then see her gone the next season.

But by the 1994 season, a whole new wave of young players had come in, and at twenty-seven I was suddenly one of the older wives. Curt and I were incredibly happy with where we were in our lives, and despite the hectic pace of everything, we both felt very ready for parenthood. Curt wanted it more than anything, especially since he was the last living male Schilling after his father died. He wanted an heir, and I would finally get the chance to be a great mother, just like my mom had been.

And that was how it happened that one minute we were a young baseball player and his wife, constantly on the go, and the next we were a family—constantly on the go.

I went into labor for the first time on the Friday night of Memorial Day weekend in 1995. After a few polite attempts to get Curt to come downstairs, I finally went to the loft where he was on the computer and shouted at him, "I'm in #$@&ing labor!" He went from the chair to the bottom of the stairs, and I'm pretty sure he didn't touch even one step on the way down.

Here was a guy who could confidently pitch in front of a hundred million people in fifty different countries without losing his nerve. But childbirth rattled him something fierce. He had to have my dad drive us to the hospital.

The next day, we gave birth to our first son. Inspired by the ALS patients we had come to know and care so much about, we named our son Gehrig Clifford Schilling. It was our way of honoring them for their courage and the life lessons they'd taught us. Lou Gehrig had an untimely death. Our little boy would bring life to the name Gehrig.

From the start, Gehrig was relatively easygoing as a baby and slept well, which made it convenient to tote him around from spring training to home to anywhere else we needed to go. He was adaptable, which was a good thing, because our life in baseball was always in flux and I felt totally discombobulated all the time. I found it difficult to keep track of where we were supposed to be and when, with everything I needed for my little baby. It took me four months just to get to the point where I was able to take a shower, feed him, and get to the ballpark in a reasonable amount of time.

Naturally we had Gehrig playing baseball from the time he could stand relatively steadily. He always enjoyed it, and also loved watching his dad play.

From a very early age, Gehrig was comfortable in our unusual world, I suppose partly because he was always so outgoing, and also because he knew how to act years beyond his age. He could easily converse with both kids and adults. If we took him into the clubhouse or to an ALS event, he'd behave himself remarkably and seem very mature, talking graciously to grown-ups when they stopped to ask him questions. He acted like he was made for this life. In my mind, he became the standard of how kids were supposed to behave in these situations. It was a standard that would complicate things later as I tried to understand Grant.

When I became pregnant with Gabby, Gehrig loved the idea of becoming a big brother. He was excited from the minute we told him I was pregnant. My water broke while Curt was on the road playing in Chicago, and eight hours later, on May 22, 1997, I gave birth to a little girl. Curt arrived just in time.

He couldn't hang around the hospital long, though. He was pitching that day. He had a few hours to go home, check on Gehrig, and grab a couple of hours' sleep before heading to the ballpark. It didn't go so well for him that day; he couldn't make it out of the second inning. All the papers had headlines such as, "Oh Baby. Schilling Can't Deliver. "

We named the baby Gabriella Patricia. She was our second—ultimately of four—to have a name beginning with *G*. No, it wasn't our favorite letter of the alphabet. We named her that because, at the time, Gabriella Sabatini was a successful tennis player, and we thought she was just the embodiment of what we wanted our daughter to be—athletic, smart, attractive, kind, and self-assured. Every teacher Gabriella has ever had has told us we named her right, because she lives up to her nickname, Gabby. She can talk and talk and talk.

As a baby, Gabriella, like Gehrig, was quite easy. She slept, woke up, ate, and went right back to sleep. You could wake her up, play with her, and put her back down without any fuss. And also like Gehrig, she was conveniently adaptable to the baseball life. You could keep her up late, and she'd just sleep later the next day. She and Gehrig really spoiled me; they made me expect Grant to be exactly the same.

Gabby is and always has been a happy girl. Her heart is huge and she is happy for everyone. She's always been a social butterfly, hard to keep at home. Right from the start, Gabby idealized her big brother. He came up with the games and she played them. Naturally, sometimes he picked on her; that's just what older siblings do. But all things considered they got along incredibly well.

The funny thing was that with one baby, I'd felt disorganized all the time, but once Gabby showed up, I became the most organized I had ever been. I figured I was getting the hang of this parenthood thing. I could take them on road trips, knowing that as long as I had a couple of action figures and books, they would stay in the stands as long as I needed them to, occasionally stopping their playing to sing "Take Me Out to the Ball Game." At home games they raced to get to the Phillies' kids' room.

The bottom line was that wherever I went with Gabby and Gehrig, it was easy. I let them know there were rules for flying, for baseball games, for parking lots. One reminder was usually all that was needed. I figured this was the way all kids were. Boy, was I in for a surprise.

TWO YEARS LATER, in spring training, we decided that we were ready for baby number three. We found out on Easter in Atlanta, with all of our family there, and I went into labor right after the season ended.

On October 13, 1999, we had the newest addition to our family, a boy. We named him Grant Ward—another name beginning with G. Well, I'd always loved the name Grant. And we were on a roll with that first initial. Ward is my dad's family's middle name, and my sister-in-law Allison's new married name was Ward. So it was a perfect name and tribute.

Now I had a four-year-old, a two-year-old, and a newborn. Let the fun begin!

Gabby and Gehrig were so excited to have another sibling. Gehrig would have a little brother, and Gabby would have a baby to care for. She was really like a second mother to Grant. When he started talking, he called me "Mommy" and her "Momma." At first I didn't realize there was a distinction. I thought he was always calling for me. But I soon found that if he said "Momma" and I answered, he'd get mad. No, he wanted Gabby, thank you very much.

Gabby mothered Grant every chance she got. When the three of them were together, there were times when they played well, and times when the older two seemed to like to make Grant scream because they could. They were all suddenly very high energy and a bit difficult to keep under control. But they were adorable, so they could get away with a lot.

Just as I was getting used to the rhythm of our life in Philly with three little kids, halfway through the 2000 baseball season, we got traded, this time to the Arizona Diamondbacks. For the first time since 1992, I had to pick up and move us more than halfway across the country—only this time I was moving a lot more than just me and two dogs. I had to push myself into high gear, quickly finding a house for us to live in, arranging for utilities to be hooked up, securing a pediatrician, packing, moving, and unpacking. My mother was able to help on the East Coast end, and she and my dad came to stay with us for the remaining two months of the season, which was a great help.

By the time they left, I was wiped out from the move. I assumed it was because of all I was juggling as an essentially single mom. But I was *really* exhausted. Like, I could barely get up some mornings. I would fall asleep if I was just sitting still. I would ask Curt a question and forget it by the time I got to the kitchen. I had always prided myself on being organized and on top of things. This made no sense at all.

"You need to go to a doctor," my mom said. My father echoed that sentiment.

"I don't have time," I said.

But then Curt chimed in and insisted I go. The regular doctor sent me to an endocrinologist. The endocrinologist discovered that I had Hashimoto's disease. Long story short: My thyroid wasn't working. I'd have to go on medication and be on it for the rest of my life.

It's a good thing I went. I don't know how long I could have kept all the balls in the air the way I needed to without addressing my health. I had a lot on my plate. Life was hectic. But it was also good. Curt and I felt blessed with three beautiful—highly active—kids, and fortunate to have the chance to continue to make this crazy baseball life work as best we could.

three
The Longest Car Ride Begins

I TELL MYSELF THE REASON I DIDN'T NOTICE ANYTHING DIF-ferent about Grant during the first few years of his life is that I was completely overwhelmed.

Gehrig and Gabby were still pretty little, so I was juggling three kids on my own almost all the time. When Grant would scream and cry and fuss in his baby seat as I drove the kids to visit Curt at spring training, I didn't stop to think, "Gee, the first two didn't cry quite as often, now did they?" I was too busy making sure everyone was dressed and fed and packed up in the car for our many road trips. I figured that chaos—and crying and screaming—were fairly normal, given our situation. I kick myself now for not paying closer attention.

As Roberto Clemente once said, baseball has been very good to me. I loved so many aspects of our life during the years Curt was playing. There were thrilling experiences—going to the World Series four times, winning three times, once with the Diamondbacks and twice with the Red Sox. Having grown up with very little, I'm very grateful for all that the game has brought into our lives and all that it has afforded me.

Still, as well versed as I'd been in moving and life alone before Curt and I had kids, nothing could have prepared me for what being a baseball wife meant once we had three kids. Having my husband essentially out of the house for eight or nine months of the year meant raising Gehrig, Gabby, and Grant mostly alone. On top of that there were all those moves. The kids would go in and out of preschools and schools, and I'd have to make sure that all the transitions went smoothly. Change was a constant in our life, and I had to stay on top of it.

I might have made things easier for myself by getting some help, but I couldn't bring myself to do that. Determined to be a great stay-at-home mother like my mom had been, I refused to get a nanny. Even though we had struggled financially when I was growing up, my mother felt it was important to be at home for us instead of getting a job. In the late seventies, when other girls showed up at school with the latest designer clothes, I remember thinking, *Why can't she go to work so I can have those things, too?* But in hindsight, I understand how valuable it was that she was there every day when my younger brother and I went off to school, and when we returned. She kept her eye out for us at all times—and for all the other kids in the neighborhood, too. She was the neighborhood matriarch, a fun mom everyone loved. She always made sure we enjoyed being kids, festively decorating the house for all the holidays, from Halloween to Christmas to Easter.

I admired the model my mother had set for me, and with three kids of my own, I felt that getting babysitters all the time or hiring a nanny would mean I wasn't living up to her image. More than that, I was self-conscious about people judging me now that I was the wife of an up-and-coming baseball player. I was uncomfortable suddenly having money, and found that it could make situations awkward and unpleasant. Sadly, some people from the past—people in our families—even stopped talking to me because of it. I still can't believe that ties were severed over money. I thought that if I had help, even more people would look at me with a mix of envy and disdain and say,

"Well, she has it *easy*. She's not doing *anything*." I cared too much about what people thought, and I felt that having help would erase everything I did as a mother in the eyes of others. So I had no babysitter, no nanny, and I took my kids with me everywhere.

What complicated things even more when Grant was little was the fact that in 2001 I received a diagnosis and intensive surgical treatment for melanoma. It started with a spot on my back. It had been there awhile. My brother and sister-in-law had each said something to me about it. I'd attempted to see a couple of different dermatologists a year or two before, when we were living in Philadelphia, but for some reason those appointments got canceled, and I didn't follow through with them. Maybe I was in denial.

At a physical in Arizona after Curt's trade, the doctor immediately noticed that spot on my back. "I don't like that," he said. "I need to remove it." I didn't think it was a big deal. I didn't argue with him and just said, "Go ahead." It seemed good to get it over with. Maybe I could even avoid the lecture about how bad the sun was for you, not to mention tanning beds. Of course, I'd heard of sunscreen and knew there was this thing called "skin cancer," but I never paid much attention to it.

I had been a serious sun worshipper. As a teen, I broiled myself on my parents' tar-covered roof, slathered in baby oil. Each season I made a point of getting a stingy red burn first, to establish a "base" for a nice tan. Just thinking about it hurts. It's amazing when you think about how much we didn't know only a short time ago. Tanning beds became a regular part of my life in my twenties. They provided a way to maintain a golden glow year-round and they were a serious time-saver for a busy person. As the technology advanced, some tanning places had the ability to administer a five-minute shot of radiation that was the equivalent of sitting in the sun for thirty minutes. I could fry myself in between the pediatrician's office and the grocery store without missing a beat. It was a way of life for me in those days. I had a perma-tan.

After removing the growth from my back, the doctor sent it to a lab for a biopsy. It never occurred to me that it might come back positive for cancer, but it did. The doctor called the next day and said I had to go see a plastic surgeon. Not only did I have skin cancer, but I had the deadly kind: melanoma. In all, I had to undergo five surgeries on my back and front to remove all the malignancy, all the while wondering, *What if they can't get it all? What if it comes back?*

Shortly after my surgeries were completed, Curt was featured in a story on ESPN because he was going to be in the 2001 All-Star game. The news of my cancer had made it around the clubhouse, and the reporter asked Curt about it. Then they sent another reporter to interview us.

At first I felt the woman wasn't taking me—or skin cancer—seriously. I felt almost mocked by her. Finally, I said to her, "I'm not going to be a part of this piece unless you show pictures." She seemed taken aback. Then I showed her pictures—like the area where they removed six inches of skin from my back. The reporter changed her tone with me. I'd finally gotten through to her.

Once ESPN ran the segment, suddenly everyone wanted to interview us. *People* magazine did a big article, and many other publications and television shows jumped on board with our human interest story.

There went my privacy. I'd barely had time to heal inside myself—I'd been too busy holding myself together for my parents and my kids. It's challenging having cancer as a relatively young person because you have living parents and small children around you and you have to be strong for them. My private inner struggle was suddenly very public. But that quickly became a blessing: I began receiving letters from people who had lost loved ones to melanoma, who felt their voices hadn't been heard. Meanwhile, I hadn't even known until my diagnosis that melanoma was deadly. It occurred to me that if I hadn't known, probably many other people didn't know, either. With that in mind, Curt and I started the SHADE Foundation, an organization dedicated to educating people about skin cancers and sun safety and raising money to provide shade coverings for playgrounds so fewer children would get melanoma.

It was an incredibly fulfilling thing, a way to take my struggle and turn it into something positive. The only problem was that it was one more thing to do; it forced me to fight even harder to keep my balance.

———————

ON CURT'S BIRTHDAY, NOVEMBER 14, 2001, he got a gift I promise you he will never get from me again: I found out I was pregnant with Garrison, our fourth child. A few weeks before Garrison was born, I was at a Diamondbacks game, talking to a few of the other wives about how busy I was. I explained to them about the five operations to treat my cancer, the charity work I was doing, and how I had to shuttle three kids to their appointments by myself, all the while being pregnant with my fourth.

"Shonda, are you crazy?" one of them said to me.

"You're killing yourself doing all of this with no help," interjected another. "What are you trying to prove?"

It was an amazingly succinct question, and one I didn't have an answer for. Just like that they had set me straight. About six weeks before delivering Garrison, I finally hired a nanny. What a difference it made. Our home was suddenly a happier place. I could spend time with my husband. The last thing I wanted was for my condition to have an impact on his performance on the field. Spending time together helped put him at ease. At last I could go to the grocery store. I could go to PTA meetings. My parents, who'd moved to Arizona to be with us and their grandkids, could go back to being grandparents instead of babysitters.

Having the nanny around also meant I could spend time with each of my kids individually. Prior to that I'd never noticed anything different about Grant. All toddlers are challenging, I thought. Grant was simply acting his age.

I FINALLY BEGAN TO NOTICE some unusual things about Grant's behavior. Grant was about three at the time, and he was moving out of the early toddler phase. He was very difficult, always saying no to everything, even to things we thought he'd want.

"Will you eat one more bite of your dinner?"

"No."

"Can you give me a hug?"

"No."

He'd even object to the things he'd said he wanted earlier.

"Let's go get ice cream."

"No."

Out of the blue, he'd have temper tantrums and throw things. He would react in an irrational, uncontrollable manner to things that made most children just a bit emotional. There had to be a logical reason, I thought. I chalked his misbehaving up to having a new little brother. Grant was suddenly no longer the baby. That had to take its toll. Now he was one of the middle children. Yes, that must be it. The problem with that logic? Gehrig hadn't had those problems when Gabby came along, and Gabby hadn't had any problem when Grant arrived. But I didn't remember any of those details at the time; it was only in hindsight that I realized how flawed my logic was.

There were other kinds of struggles. Grant had a phobia about trying anything new. I couldn't get him to try catching a ball with a glove. I couldn't get him to try ice-skating. If there was any chance that he would fail at something, he wouldn't even go near it. There was no coaxing him into it. He would dig his heels in and shout, *"No!"*

Driving long distances with Grant was a nightmare, and we had to do that often, to go visit Curt on the road. I liked to get silly with the kids and turn up the radio. The others liked to sing songs with me and do crazy dances as we drove. But Grant would have none of it.

"*Turn it off! Turn it off! Turn it off!*" he'd scream at the top of his lungs. He would scream the entire time. The rest of us would get mad at him because he was just killing a fun family moment.

I'd scream right back at him. "*You do not dictate what happens in this car!*" I'd say. He'd keep at it, though.

"*Turn it off! Turn it off! Turn it off!*"

I didn't know what to do. Here I was, driving these kids for two hours each way every weekend to go see Curt at spring training, and there was now no way for me to make it fun and to help the time pass. He'd also go crazy if the other kids wanted to watch a different DVD than he did on the player in the minivan. It wasn't just that he'd disagree. He'd have a total meltdown, crying and screaming. I always felt bad about giving in to him, yet I'd still cave. I knew it wasn't fair at all to the other kids, but it was the only way to calm Grant down.

Those rides were awful. I would keep thinking, *Let me just get through these two hours.* Usually I'd been alone with the kids all week. I was so eager to hand them over to Curt and have a little break—I can't even describe how badly I needed a break. Even going to the grocery store by myself seemed like a treat. Just an hour without Grant challenging me, without any yelling from him or at him, and without the others whining about Grant, was a blessing.

For some reason, I would always find myself crying in the frozen foods section, though I don't think it had anything to do with the particular selection there. It was more that it took me a little while to get to that aisle, and by that point, after hearing a few of those sentimental oldies songs they always seem to play in the supermarket, my emotions would have gotten the better of me. It just seemed like the frozen food aisle was where it all came crashing down each week. Grant, the kids, baseball—all of it. I would cry and cry as I shopped, trying not to look anyone in the eye, and hoping people didn't notice.

———•———

As GARRISON GREW, it only emphasized the ways in which Grant's early years had been out of step. By the time Garrison was just fifteen months old, it began to dawn on me that he was much easier than Grant had been, even at that early age. It was the fall of 2003, and as Garrison was toddling around, I noticed there were certain ways he behaved—and listened—that made it clearer that Grant was different.

As I had with Gehrig and Gabby, I instituted a rule that no matter where we were or what we were doing, if I said, "Freeze!" they had to stop and stand in place quietly. Grant had always been immune to "Freeze!" and I assumed it meant I was losing my touch as a parent. Maybe I was simply stretched too thin. But then Garrison came along and crushed that theory.

As soon as I said "Freeze!" to Garrison, he got it. He just stopped and froze. He didn't question me. He just stood in place, and seemed to know it was for his own good. Meanwhile, Grant would keep running around. And around. And around. While he ran around, he also made a point of touching whatever he could possibly get his hands on. It's a parent's worst nightmare— a kid putting his hands on literally everything, putting himself potentially in harm's way and also messing things up in the house. It seemed that no amount of childproofing was sufficient when Grant was around.

Grant also couldn't handle even a little bit of teasing by his older siblings. Kids tease—it's what they do. But Grant reacted to it as if it were a life-threatening event. He would run and hide behind the large curtains in our kitchen and stay there forever. If the kids ratcheted it up a notch, he would go into a high-pitched frenzy, at times almost tearing the curtains from the ceiling. Needless to say, it would ruin everyone's day.

While I noticed differences like this, I didn't make too much of them. Grant was proving himself to be his own person, I thought. Sure, he was harder to control than his siblings, but still he was an incredibly kind and generous child.

Complicating things in that fall of 2003 was the fact that there was only a year left on Curt's contract, and we knew our time was up with the Diamondbacks. A trade was going to happen sooner or later, but the Diamondbacks management could not make any decisions without Curt's say-so. Curt had something called a no-trade clause in his contract, which stipulated that the management could not trade him without his consent. We'd heard whispers of a deal with the New York Yankees, which I would have been fine with because that meant going back to my beloved East Coast. Even if we were traded to the Yankees, we would still be able to live in Philly. We had just sold our house in Philadelphia and bought a new one with the plan to live there after Curt retired. Moving to the Yankees would have allowed us to start living there sooner rather than later.

On November 23, we had a big event at our house for the SHADE Foundation that I'd been working on for months. It didn't matter that it was my birthday—I worked all day. The party went well. The house was beautiful, and we had tables with candles set up out by the pool. One of the forty or so guests was Jerry Colangelo, who at the time was the owner of the Diamondbacks. He had been incredibly supportive of the SHADE Foundation from the beginning, and in addition to being a generous donor, he was instrumental in getting other people in Arizona signed on to help. However, that night at the party something about him kept distracting me. Throughout the night, he and Curt kept disappearing and talking secretively.

"What's going on?" I finally said, poking my nose into Curt's office, where they were talking alone. The two of them just smiled mischievously.

"I'm trading you," Mr. Colangelo joked, and Curt found this hilarious. Ha, ha, ha. They were like two little bad boys plotting something that they might get in trouble for.

Despite this strange behavior on their part, by the end of the night we had raised two hundred thousand dollars, which meant we could build at least twenty more shade covers, a huge number for us. When it was all over, everyone left except the twelve people who had been most involved in helping me plan the event. I stood on a chair in my kitchen and thanked them all. Then my husband stood on the chair.

"We're getting traded to the Red Sox!" he announced.

My jaw dropped. *"The Red Sox?"* I yelled. *"Where the hell did that come from?"*

The answer was simple: At the party, Mr. Colangelo had asked Curt's permission to trade us, Curt agreed, and then Mr. Colangelo told him that they had already begun working on a deal to trade us to the Red Sox. He couldn't have timed it any better.

Ordinarily this kind of decision would not have been announced or decided at a charity dinner, but Curt has never been one to do things in an ordinary kind of way. He didn't have agents, and in his contract decisions he represented himself with a little help from me. When Curt and I finally spoke after the last of the guests had left, he told me that Red Sox president Larry Lucchino, general manager Theo Epstein, and assistant general manager Jed Hoyer were coming to talk to us—the next day!

To add to the chaos, I was getting ready to cook my first Thanksgiving dinner. It was going to be a full house: my parents, my brother Michael with his wife Shelby and their new daughter, Delaney, and Curt's cousin Clarence and his family would all be joining us.

On Monday morning, the call came that the Boston management wanted to visit with us. We were taken aback by the TV trucks stationed outside our house, and the group of journalists waiting for an answer or comment. We hadn't expected that. We didn't exactly have the best setup for privacy, either—just a fence on one side of our U-shaped house. The only way to get from our bedroom and office to the kitchen and family room was down a long hallway of nothing but windows. Every move we made was on display for everyone to see.

Late that afternoon we received a letter from the Red Sox saying how excited they were to meet us. Ready or not, our next journey was about to begin. Curt asked my mother to watch the kids and he took me to the Red Lobster so we could talk privately about what we thought of moving to Boston and what we would ask for in a contract, since we would be handling it ourselves. Lobster seemed like the right meal for considering a move to New England.

The next day, Tuesday, as my brother and his family pulled up to our house, so did the Red Sox executives, as well as Larry Lucchino's wife, Stacey, who came to answer any questions I might have. The circus was about to begin. The men presented Curt with a very well-thought-out plan, with charts and visuals illustrating why he'd be such a perfect fit. They had data that supported why Curt would have so much success in Fenway Park. Touching my heart, they even had a folder with a plan for how they'd help us further our campaigns for ALS and the SHADE Foundation. We thanked them for coming and said we would meet them on Wednesday.

We met with them for hours on Wednesday. It was intense. Curt and I would bring up the things we wanted, and they would mention the things they needed. Then they would go to our basement and talk, and we would go to our office and talk. It was crazy, looking back on it. Curt and I were a team, bouncing ideas off one another and trying different approaches. If we were going to force our family to move once again, we needed to make sure it was worth it in every way for the kids and for us.

I have to say, while pretty much every athlete has an agent these days, there is an advantage to doing your own negotiating. When you're representing yourself, team owners aren't going to say, "Your client isn't worth that much, he has a bad attitude, and his ERA has sucked for the past two years," because they're not negotiating with an agent—they're negotiating with you. What came out of both sides was nice, although we had some heated moments.

Often there's a power play that happens between agent and owner, and sometimes comments are taken out of context or repeated differently to the client. There's no chance of this when you're sitting right there in front of the people you're negotiating with. Along the same lines, we never would have been negotiating in our living room if there'd been an agent involved. I had deliberately invited them into our home for the negotiations so that all the trophies and magazine covers—including the World Series trophy from the 2001 win with the Diamondbacks—would be in front of their eyes, like dangling meat in front of a tiger.

At the end of Wednesday, the negotiations weren't completed. Larry and Stacey departed for Thanksgiving in San Diego. That left Theo and Jed. These two men with no family in Arizona were destined to spend Thanksgiving in a hotel room. But there was no way we were going to let that happen. Curt insisted they eat dinner with us, or the deal was off.

Naturally news of this meal with Red Sox management made its way to the sports media, which my mom found incredibly amusing. "I have been cooking Thanksgiving for thirty years," she said. "You cook one, and it's in every newspaper."

"Great," I thought to myself. "Now, if the deal falls through, the whole Red Sox Nation will blame it on my first attempt at cooking turkey."

Jed and Theo showed up for dinner. We ate, and then got right back into the contract negotiations. The grown-ups were watching football. There were kids running around all over the place. Things were business as usual in the Schilling house, as far as the kids knew. Curt and I kept breaking away from everyone to work out the deal with them.

Now we were getting to the money part. That was sticky and uncomfortable. We realized that a certain number they put out there was a lot of money, but it was a low number compared to what comparable players were paid. It was tempting, but we realized that if Curt accepted less than what he was aiming for, it would affect other players who had earned that money. When players go through negotiations, they compare other players' salaries with their time in the big leagues and accomplishments. It sets the bar for what players can ask for.

Unfortunately, they didn't go for our number. When Theo and Jed left that night, we believed it was over. We couldn't reach an agreement. Sadly, Curt and I had already hooked ourselves into the adventure of moving to Boston. But we were millions away. They'd offered $10 million for the 2004 season, but the market said Curt was worth $14 million.

The kids required an altogether different set of negotiations. They felt they had total no-trade clauses. They had their friends, they had the beginnings of roots and routines that they all loved. Moving would be an especially big challenge for Grant because, unlike the other three, he thrived on familiarity and routine. Without those comforts, he often freaked out.

So we broke out the big guns: snow days! The kids instantly gave up their no-trade clauses upon realizing that the weather could actually keep them out of school.

With our kids on board, we gave it one more shot on Friday afternoon. Larry returned to Arizona for this meeting. Curt and I were on the phone with our lawyer and we came up with $12 million and a $2 million bonus if they won the World Series. That would bridge our gap. It was our last shot.

Larry interjected, "We can't go above ten million."

That's when I spoke up. "Hey, I don't have a problem going to New York," I said. "We're not signing a contract for ten million dollars." I had to stand up and say that. While we believed Boston was a good fit, Curt's career was the lifeblood of our family; everything we did was about the best place to play baseball for us.

We broke once again. When we got back together, the deal was done: $12 million and a $2 million World Series bonus. Everyone got on the phone and called someone. The press conference was set up for that night. We were traded to Boston and introduced to Red Sox Nation. Life would never be the same again.

In all these negotiations, of course, there were always lingering questions in the back of my mind about how the kids would react to such a dramatic change. They'd accepted the snow days, but I knew Grant was less than enthusiastic for reasons the other kids never thought of. Above all, his attachments to his teacher and friends were unusually strong for a kid his age. This was going to be a challenge.

four
A Control Problem Comes to Boston

ONCE AGAIN WE WERE MAKING A BIG MOVE. THIS TIME IT WAS with four kids. As usual, we had to act quickly. Curt left for spring training in early 2004, moving to Florida for seven weeks with my dad. Meanwhile, my mom and I stayed behind and packed up the house.

This was the first time we'd had to pick up and leave since Gehrig, Gabby, and Grant had gotten a bit older, and this made the process of saying goodbye a lot harder. During the move to Arizona, all three had been young enough that relocating was a relatively tear-free ordeal. Now, though Garrison was still young, the others had all developed friendships and routines in Arizona that would make this a much more difficult transition.

It would be hardest for Grant because of his aversion to changes in people or environment—not to mention trying new things. Our new home posed unique, Grant-related challenges for us, too. For example, our house in Arizona was very open and had very few doors, which made it easy to explain to Grant which doors he could and could not go through. Our house in Boston had as many doors on one floor as there were in the entire Arizona house. Knowing that it would be more difficult to keep Grant from wandering and exploring on his own scared the hell out of me. I couldn't childproof fast enough.

There wasn't a lot of time for us to fuss over finding the home of our dreams—we just needed a house big enough for all of us, and one where we could have some privacy. We'd been warned that some Red Sox fans could be very aggressive about approaching players and their families, and we wanted to have at least a bit of a buffer from that.

With Grant, though, it was becoming increasingly difficult to maintain that buffer in public. He gave me a hard time no matter where we were, and when we were out, it called attention to us. For some reason, he was more difficult with me than he was with Curt, my parents, or babysitters. Even though Garrison was younger, it was Grant I worried more about if we were away from home.

Parking lots were a particular source of anxiety for me. Grant was a wanderer with virtually no fear of anything. He was easily distracted, and if we were walking somewhere, he'd head off to whatever had caught his attention. If we walked in a parking lot and I asked him to hold my hand, he would say no. Then when I reached for his hand, he would move away just far enough so I couldn't get him. If I did get hold of his hand or his shoulder, he would wriggle, trying to get loose. And sometimes he'd run away from me with no regard for or awareness of the cars everywhere, causing me to have mini-heart attacks as I fought off visions of him being run over.

I screamed at him so many times. Looking back, I don't know how I might have handled it differently. When it came to his safety, I saw no other choice than to protect him as best I could, and so I would dig my heels in—which meant yelling. In the meantime, with Grant commanding so much of my attention, I was left to rely on my older kids—Gehrig was then nine, and Gabby was seven—to supervise Garrison in his stroller and make sure he was safe. That in itself should have told me that something was not right with this setup.

At some point after the arrival in Boston, I made a conscious decision to avoid situations where Grant and I would be walking around in public. In addition to his safety, I was also concerned about making a scene. If I yelled at him, I called attention to myself and to him, and with the increased scrutiny of our family that came along with Curt's playing in Boston, there was nothing I dreaded more than calling attention to ourselves. I'd always been too preoccupied with what people thought about me, and never was that truer than when we first arrived in Boston. My self-consciousness had reached new highs. I was constantly worried about whether people were silently judging me—not just as a parent, but as a wife of a star pitcher on their beloved Red Sox.

While Grant's inability to stay focused was dangerous in public, the flip side was that when he zeroed in on something, he'd get hyperfocused, and there was no way of breaking his concentration. If we were in a store, and there was something that appealed to him, I couldn't get him out of that store until I parted with my money and got him what he wanted. If we were in an airport that had one of those play areas for kids, it could be a mixed blessing for me. On the one hand, I could occupy Grant there the whole time we were waiting for a plane to take off. On the other hand, if we didn't have time for him to play, and we needed to hustle to get onto our plane, I was in big trouble.

This happened that first year with the Red Sox, when Grant was four. We were on our way to visit Curt at spring training, and we were in a hurry. I had Grant and Garrison in strollers, and Gehrig and Gabby were walking alongside me. We were racing to the gate, but then Grant caught sight of the play area. That was it.

He tore off, out of his stroller, and ran to play. I ran after him, all the other kids in tow. "Grant, we have to go now," I said. "We have to go catch the plane."

No kid wants to leave that play area filled with toys and airplanes and a make-believe control tower. Grant simply refused. *"No!"* he shouted at me.

"Grant," I repeated, kneeling down and trying to get him to look me in the eye. That never seemed to work. "We'll play another time. We have to catch the plane now."

"No! No! No!"

Of course, now all the other parents have turned their heads and are staring at us. For the life of me, I can't get Grant out of the play area and back into the stroller. He's just quick enough at that age that I can't easily grab him—not to mention that I've got three other kids to keep my eye on and usher to the gate.

With everyone watching, I grabbed his hand and tried to discreetly get him out of there. But he wasn't going to make it easy.

"You're hurting me!" he yelled. *"You're hurting me! Stop hurting me!"*

So now all the parents and other flyers stood there staring, clearly under the impression that they were witnessing child abuse, and quietly inching their hands toward their cell phones to call the authorities. I didn't know what to do, because we couldn't miss our plane. I was so uncomfortable with the glares I was receiving as I dragged Grant to the gate.

In the past, when people would witness him misbehaving or freaking out in public, and then hear us scolding him loudly, I would cringe, suspecting they thought he was uncontrollable and that we had no discipline in our home. I would have assumed the same thing at one time. I recall being a very young mother—maybe only Gehrig had been born so far—and watching as someone's kid pitched a fit in the supermarket cereal aisle because he wasn't allowed to have the cereal he wanted. His mother got into a screaming match with him, and then he just lay down on the floor, sobbing and wailing. All I could think was *Why can't she get control of her kid? He clearly has no respect for her.* I didn't know who I thought was more of a problem, the child or the mother. That was then.

Standing there in the airport with my hand on Grant's shoulder, the only word for what I felt was *failure*. I didn't know how to reach my kid. But also, I apparently hadn't earned his respect. When I was a kid, if my mother grabbed me under the back of my hair, that was it. I knew I had to fall in line. Heck, she could just look at me a certain way and I'd know I had to behave better.

The other kids got it. If I said to them, "We don't have time today to play before the flight," they understood. Maybe one of them would whine a little, but that was the extent of it. They knew I was in charge, and they could figure out the reasoning behind what I was saying: We're trying not to be late.

Once we got to wherever we were going—visiting Curt, or taking a vacation—a whole new set of challenges awaited us. The one good thing about traveling was that Grant liked hotel rooms. Before we'd leave home, he'd put up a fight about going, but once we got to the hotel room, he was a happy camper. He'd watch TV, play video games, order the foods he knew he loved from room service. Of course the downside was that getting him out of the room was always difficult, even if we were going to the pool, which he loved— a little too much.

Eventually I'd get him there, though, and he'd immediately make his presence known. Everyone at every pool we've ever gone to has gotten to know Grant's name. That's because I always have to say things like, *"Stop jumping in, Grant!"* and *"Grant, stop running around the pool!"* and *"Grant, stop splashing people!"* Soon all the other adults in the vicinity are chanting *"Grant!"* every five minutes, trying to get him to stop doing something or other.

He was always big on slides. We took the kids to Disney World in Florida once, and he got superfocused on the slide at the pool. He loved shooting down it and into the water. Every time he came out of the pool, he went right up to the top—cutting in front of everyone else in line. Naturally, no one was happy about that. But Grant didn't seem to notice. He was oblivious to the fact that everyone was mad at him. He just kept going up the slide until he got kicked off, and then came crying to me.

A few months later we took the kids to Puerto Rico, and again Grant wasn't sharing the slide with others. (Come to think of it, he has probably gotten kicked off every pool slide he's ever gotten on.) I kept watching, but after a while I stopped seeing him go down the slide. I thought to myself, *Where the heck is Grant?* And then I got up and looked for him. He was sitting in the chair at the top of the slide.

"What's he doing up there?" I asked the lifeguard, a young woman in her twenties.

"I gave him a time-out," she casually informed me. "He wasn't sharing."

I went berserk. Who was this lifeguard to punish my son? I told her, "I will correct my own child," although she clearly thought I wasn't doing a very good job of that. I was completely humiliated. I went to the head of the resort and complained. "She will never take it upon herself to correct my child again," I said.

But deep down, I understood the lifeguard's frustration. I felt embarrassed that Grant had brought her to that point. I had no idea why he was so difficult to control, why he didn't listen. To me, it was some sort of weakness on my part as a parent, or the effect of the chaotic baseball-family lifestyle. The idea that it was something more fundamental, more ingrained, and more serious never even crossed my mind.

———•———

WE HAD BEEN IN Massachusetts just two weeks when the 2004 season started. Life always becomes even more hectic during the season, and this year did not fail to deliver. The season started out with a bang. I had never been to a stadium that had so much energy, every day. The Red Sox fans had such incredible enthusiasm it was infectious.

The kids were in school and making friends. I started coaching Gabby in softball, and Gehrig played baseball. When it got to be summer, we would go to the games every night, and usually I'd put the kids in the family room, which Grant in particular enjoyed. I was one of the older wives on the team, so I had older kids than most. This meant that there were plenty of babies and toddlers around in the family room. Most kids on the cusp of five are too busy with other kids their age, or with their own toys, to notice kids littler than themselves. Not Grant, though. He loved little kids, and he only wanted to take care of them. This was what made the family room so much fun for him. With the adult supervision provided there, he was able to be involved with the babies, and no one had to worry about him hurting them in any way. Grant would stay there through an entire game, and I could watch Curt pitch without feeling as if I had to go though a wrestling match in order to do it.

Shortly after we arrived in Boston, I put Grant into a preschool there, and when I heard he had a new best friend I was thrilled. What got complicated were the playdates. I knew that both Gehrig and Gabby could do playdates; they'd been doing them for years. But with Grant I wasn't so sure how it would go. Needless to say, I had my reservations, and I was not all that eager to introduce playdates to Grant. But once he'd known that little boy for a couple of months and since they played together so well every day at school, I figured it wouldn't hurt to try a playdate for ninety minutes or so. I called the little boy's mom and made arrangements.

Grant was overwhelmed with anticipation. He couldn't stop talking about how he was going to have a playdate, what he was going to do on the playdate, how much fun the playdate was going to be. I must have heard the word *playdate* about fifty times within a three-day span.

The day arrived, and the little boy came over. He and Grant immediately took off to play. After fifteen minutes, though, I looked over to the family room and saw Grant by himself on the couch, watching TV alone.

"Grant!" I scolded him. "You have a friend over! When a friend comes over, you have to play with him." Grant barely reacted. He acted as if the little boy was not even there.

"Go back upstairs and play with him!" I said. And he went. After a while I went upstairs to check on them. Sure enough, Grant was in his room reading.

Now the way I understood it, when your child has a playdate, it's supposed to keep him busy and occupied. It's supposed to be easy for the mom.

But here I was, having to work harder than if I'd been home with Grant alone.

After a little more time of being ignored, the little boy asked if he could go home. Grant just wouldn't play with him, no matter how many times I asked Grant to come in the room and play. He kept saying, "No!"

I felt caught. I didn't know what to do. Was I really going to call this little boy's mother and tell her, "Your son wants to go home because my son doesn't know how to have friends over"?

I couldn't imagine what Grant was thinking. I never had to go over what a playdate was with Gabby and Gehrig. I was already keeping Grant from going over to other friends' houses because I feared he wouldn't listen. After this playdate, I was certain he wouldn't be going anywhere for a long time.

AS WE ALL SETTLED into our new routines in Boston, I became increasingly aware of something I'd suspected for a long time: Curt's relationship with Grant was incredibly tense. In truth, I'd seen this building and developing for a while, but it was not until our lives were disrupted by the move that I began to see just how strained things had become.

Not surprisingly, it hadn't been like this with either of Grant's older siblings. With Gehrig, Curt had always had a very good, natural bond, bordering on a friendship. Gehrig was Curt's link back to his own father. Curt had been the only boy in his family, and his father had been his best friend—the voice of reason that helped Curt figure things out after he'd made a bad choice or felt like he just needed to talk. There were many passions that Curt shared with his dad, but most importantly, he had tremendous respect for him. Curt's father held him accountable for his actions, and as a result, when he was growing up, the thought of disappointing his father was more upsetting to him than any punishment he could have been given.

I often think that Curt was misunderstood in baseball, from the time he started out. It had a lot to do with losing his dad just as he was getting going in the game. Curt missed that voice that would help him navigate life's big decisions. He was twenty-one and had just made it to the big leagues. He was making money and acting like an immature twenty-one-year-old. He was getting a taste of stardom and money, and he was labeled "wild" and "out of control." I think he was just lost, and longing for his dad. Imagine the pressure of moving into the big leagues without your beacon of light, in this case, Curt's dad, to talk to.

There are certain people who are hard to replace. His father was larger than life, and nothing had been able to replace that one vital relationship. But when Gehrig came along, he helped fill the hole left by Curt's father. It was perfect. Gehrig loved his daddy, he loved baseball, and he was willing to play whatever game Curt wanted to play. He went to the ballpark with him. He went on road trips. In fact, in those days Gehrig often spent more time with Curt than I was able to.

Then came Gabby. She was the princess. All she had to do to get her daddy's love was climb in Curt's lap. Curt was seemingly incapable of yelling at her, or saying no to her. She knew that even though Curt didn't crawl on the floor and wrestle with her the way he did with Gehrig, he still worshipped her. Gabby never really needed much from anyone anyway. She loved everyone, and didn't worry about how much time any one person spent with her.

When Grant came along, it was a different story. Curt was good with Grant as a baby, but Grant was the third. It was the classic birth order story: You take tons of pictures with the first, a few with the second, and barely any with the third. Curt and I didn't love Grant any less, of course, but the novelty of parenthood had been eclipsed by the day-to-day realities of having three kids and a crazy baseball-centric family life.

The other kids played with Grant, so there was plenty of attention to go around for him—even if there wasn't as much coming from his dad—and when Grant was about three, it became clear that he didn't care whether he had Curt's approval or not. A relationship with Grant meant you had to work. He argued constantly, pouted a lot, and had big, loud, messy meltdowns. He was a different kind of child than the other two had been, for sure. It required more effort on Curt's part, and sadly there wasn't much payoff for his effort. Grant seemed aloof no matter what Curt did, and Curt's time was limited.

Part of the problem with Grant was that he didn't always seem to have respect for adults—and that included Curt and me. Because of Curt's relationship with his father, respect was critically important to him, and this complicated his interactions with Grant. Curt thought like I did—old school. When our parents yelled, they had our attention and we respected them. We figured it would be the same with our kids, so when they weren't behaving, we yelled. For the most part, the others responded to that. But not Grant. He wouldn't listen, and then we'd have to resort to measures that would make him melt down. If Curt grabbed him by the arm, Grant would scream as if Curt were killing him. We had no idea what to make of it. It was a big mess. Grant couldn't see that Curt was angry. Meanwhile, Curt was hell-bent on getting control of his kid, no matter what. To make matters worse, Grant would get nervous when being scolded, and he would let out this nervous giggle that could make you twice as mad.

When Grant was hurt, he wanted nothing to do with Curt. I can imagine that was painful for Curt. It was tough on me, too. I was exhausted from being the one Grant wanted all day. I was the constant in Grant's life. I was safe. I wasn't going anywhere, unlike Curt, who was away so much.

By the time we got to Boston, it was very clear to me that Curt and Grant weren't close, and it bothered me. Not knowing any better at the time, I thought Curt wasn't trying. I knew that it couldn't be easy, but I thought that if he would only put time into Grant, they would eventually click the way he and Gehrig did. I leaned on Curt a little to try and get him to make the first moves. I wanted him to take Grant to the ballpark with him. But when I finally managed to convince Curt to take Grant to the ballpark, Grant refused to go, which of course frustrated me no end. Here I was fighting for him and he didn't care. I wanted them to spend time together, but it was so much work that Curt would yell loudly at him and Grant would completely shut down.

Occasionally, Grant would agree to go with Curt to the clubhouse, but it didn't go too well. Grant elicited mixed feelings from the other players there. They all loved him because he was so adult when he spoke with them, but they were also wary of him because his behavior was so random and unpredictable.

Since Grant had no interest in going to the batting cage or on the field, Curt would take him into the room where the players relaxed, which was off-limits to anyone besides players and their kids. They'd hang out and play Xbox for a while, which was okay. Then when it came time for Curt to go to the training room or get ready for batting practice, he would walk Grant through the rules: no running around, no wandering, no touching other people's stuff. Sure enough, thirty minutes later Curt would find him wandering around the training room, touching people's things. Curt had always found it disrespectful when other players and their wives brought their kids to the clubhouse and let them roam and do whatever they wanted. He didn't want to be that guy, or have Grant be that kid, but with Grant it felt like they were, which understandably made Curt more reluctant to take him there.

———•———

WATCHING YOUR TEAM PLAY again and again is not a hard thing to do when the team is winning, and that season we were winning. It was thrilling to be there. Curt made the All-Star team that year, and we went off to Houston. Then, before I knew it, the kids were heading back to school.

We made it to the playoffs. The first round was against the California Angels. Not a lot of wives went on the road trip. I guess that's what happens when you make it to the playoffs often—it's not such a big deal. After two quick wins, we were back home. Next stop: the Yankees.

Now it's one thing to imagine that legendary, almost one-hundred-year-old rivalry from afar. It's another to witness it with your own eyes. After the tragic 2003 American League Championship when the Yankees won in the bottom of the fourteenth inning on a home run, the Red Sox fans begged for the rematch. Me, I would rather have gone an easier route. Not to mention that the odds were not in our favor. It had been eighty-six years since the Red Sox won a World Series. What was the chance that we'd come out on top?

It was an exciting time to be in Boston, and it was fun to see my kids get swept up in the excitement generated by the Red Sox Nation. The playoffs, and the possibility of going to the World Series, were all they could talk about. Grant didn't really know what to make of it all. He was just very concerned about making sure he had a Red Sox shirt to wear to school on Red Sox Spirit Day, like his teachers told him to. He was very glad he had something to wear for it. Of course, he didn't realize that half his wardrobe was Red Sox gear. For him, the playoffs had another upside: They meant that he didn't have to say good-bye for the winter to all his friends in the Red Sox playroom.

The first three games did not get off to a good start, and just like that we were in the hole three games to none in the best-of-seven series. Curt didn't have a good start in the first game. He was having trouble with his ankle. One of his tendons was torn. By the time we went to New York, where he would pitch game six, his doctors had the crazy idea of sewing the tendon down to keep it from dislocating. No one had any idea whether or not it would work. He came back to our hotel room the night before he pitched, and I honestly thought I would throw up. He had these four big stitches on his ankle, and lord knows what they were attached to. The whole thing was puffy and had fresh wounds on it.

"How in the world are you going to pitch?" I asked him.

He just looked at me. Clearly, in his mind, there was no other choice. I couldn't imagine any part of the body not being sore after it was cut open. Still, wounded foot or not, we both somehow felt incredibly calm when Curt left for the ballpark the next day. It was the calmest either of us had ever felt before a game. It was a sense of being in the zone, and knowing that when things are going well, anything can happen.

Needless to say, Curt and the team delivered a magical night, but because I was up in the stands, it wasn't until my sister-in-law Allison called that I knew what everyone had been watching all night.

"His foot is bleeding!" she said. "They keep showing his foot on television." I had horrible visions of those stitches being ripped out and that ankle swollen something fierce. But there was too much excitement for Curt to worry about his foot. Something special was in the air.

Even though we were winning by a lot, the wives from last year knew better than to relax. They had been in the same exact situation the year before when the Yankees had won. There would be no such fate for our rivals from New York this year. We went on to win game six, which Curt had pitched, as well as the decisive game seven the following day.

When the last out was made the celebration began, but it didn't last long, because we had to get on a plane and go home. Later that night I asked Curt, "Hey, where's the sock?"

"I threw it in the garbage!" He hadn't realized that the whole world had been focused on that sock.

Next stop: the World Series against the St. Louis Cardinals. The first two games were at home. The Sox went ahead the first game and were up in the series 1–0. Everyone around us was thrilled. I had never seen so much excitement over a team in all my years in baseball. People put up signs all over our driveway and actually set up lawn chairs at the end of it. Homemade signs were posted by locals along the entire route Curt would travel to the ballpark—signs that read, "Bring us a ring, we will make you king!" The kids' playground at school was a sea of Red Sox shirts.

Curt decided to do the surgery one more time. He was in pain and uncomfortable, which was to be expected considering that the procedure was performed on a table in the clubhouse, but the night before he was to pitch again,

Curt and I stuck to his routine so that he could get into game mode. Mostly that meant him going to bed late, then reading reports in the morning and getting his game face ready. I put the kids to bed and went to bed myself. No matter how much fun the World Series might be, I still had to get enough sleep because the kids had to be at school in the morning.

I woke up at 6 A.M. that morning to find Curt wide awake and staring at me, which was very unusual for him on the morning of a game.

"What's wrong?" I asked.

"I'm in so much pain," he replied, "I can't walk. I was up the whole night. My ankle is swollen and it's killing me."

"Why didn't you wake me?" I begged.

"I didn't want you to not sleep either," he said.

It was frightening enough to see Curt up before noon on a day when he was pitching. But to see him in sheer agony left me feeling helpless.

"Who can I call?" I offered. "What do you need me to do?"

I had been with this man for fifteen years. I knew two things for certain: one, he wanted more than anything to pitch, and two, he must really be in pain if he was up this early. I got him some pain medicine and put an ice pack on his ankle. He called the trainer, told him there was no way he would be able to pitch that night, and went back to sleep. When he woke at one in the afternoon, he was still in agony.

"Is there anything I can do?" I asked him.

"I just have to go to the ballpark," he said. "I'm so uncomfortable, there's no way I'm going to pitch. I can't even walk."

I carried his stuff to the car and he left. There were none of the usual good-luck kisses, none of the silly, rhymie little poems I liked to give him to make him laugh. He looked like a kid who'd been waiting all week to go to the carnival and got sick on the day. I tried to think of something to lift his spirits, but I knew deep down that there was nothing I could do. I knew it was going to kill him to go down the driveway and come across the fans holding their signs, waiting to wave him good-bye. It was cool for me to see them, and I wasn't even pitching, but in Curt's state that day, he probably felt like he was about to let them all down, and that must have hurt.

I worried about him all day. I went to the ballpark that night and called over to the clubhouse. "I'm just checking on Curt," I said. "How's he doing?"

"He's doing great!" said Jack McCormick, the traveling secretary. "He's in the bull pen warming up."

What? I swear, World Series or not, I wanted to choke Curt. The first two innings, I was furious that he couldn't find a minute to call and say he was okay. But then there was so much excitement, I forgot I was angry at him. It was freezing at the ballpark that night, but that didn't dampen the energy in the stands. Curt pitched a gem, and we were up 2–0 in the series. He was told the camera had been fixed on his ankle the last game, so he decided that if he bled again, which he probably would, he would write "KALS" on his sock so the ALS patients would know he was thinking of them. ("K" stands for "strike-out.")

It happened, and he did it. I think it's one of the smartest things he has ever done. The awareness he raised for ALS was unbelievable. And he managed to hang on to that sock. It now resides in the Baseball Hall of Fame. My parents had to drive it there because no one would insure it in transit. The stains are really not that big, but the story is.

After the game, Curt walked into the wives' room. I started crying, and he teared up, too.

"We did it!" he said to me. "We did it!"

It was a great moment and I was relieved and happy, but then I looked at him sternly. "You couldn't find one minute to call me?" I said. "I've been sick over you all day."

"I'm so sorry," he said plaintively. But two seconds later he was back to ecstatic. "We did it!"

We said good-bye to our kids and boarded the plane to St. Louis. In St. Louis we won the next game to go up 3–0 on the Cardinals. All we needed now was one more victory to be World Series champions. And so it was that with two outs in the bottom of the ninth inning, Keith Foulke tossed the ball to first and it was all over. Boston had waited eighty-six years for this. I could only begin to imagine what joy this would bring to that city. We celebrated in the clubhouse for a couple of hours, and once again we were on a flight back to Boston. No one could sleep, even though it was five in the morning.

Apparently no one in Boston slept either. They lined the streets of our bus route, from the airport to the stadium. Being on the field in St. Louis had been nothing like seeing the Red Sox fans' reaction to this memorable series. Everyone was exhausted—teachers, kids, parents. People had woken their kids up to see history being made. I'd seen Curt play a lot of ball in a lot of different places since we'd first met, but I'd never seen anything like this.

five
The Trouble with "Circle Time"

※

THE KIDS TOOK WELL TO BOSTON, ESPECIALLY AFTER THE 2004 World Series and the enthusiastic reception we all got from the Red Sox Nation. It took awhile for the excitement to settle down, but when it did, my attention was drawn to things I'd been missing—namely, Grant's increasingly problematic behavior.

Now that he was getting older, we expected that he would be easier to get through to, and that he would listen when he was told to behave in certain ways. But that wasn't happening. In the fall of 2005, his kindergarten teacher told us that she couldn't get him to join in with the other kids in the regular morning gathering on the rug.

"He refuses to come sit with the class for 'circle time,'" she said to me. This made no sense to Curt and me. We had tried to instill in all our kids that you listen to adults who are in charge. We couldn't understand why Grant was disrespecting his teacher. I went back to his preschool to ask whether he'd given them a hard time about that, and his teacher there told me the same thing.

"Yeah," she said, "he never wanted to come to circle time. He fought us on that."

We sat Grant down to talk about it, but it wasn't easy. He was looking all over the place. When you talk to Grant, if the subject matter isn't one he's interested in, he refuses to make eye contact beyond a blink. He's always been that way.

"Grant," I said, trying to hold his gaze, "until you are willing to sit in circle time every day, we're taking away your Littlest Pet Shop toys." At the time, he collected these little magnetic toys. He had buckets full of them. He was always collecting tiny little things. Without hesitation, Grant burst into tears. He cried and cried—to the point that you'd think he'd just lost his best friend. It seemed as if he was overreacting, which he did, often. But he was so affected by the loss of those toys that he finally went to circle time.

And yet at the same time that he struggled with listening to adults at school, he displayed a level of caring and understanding that was far beyond his years. That year in kindergarten, Grant started removing my purse from my shoulder and carrying it for me. He would also open doors for me. I couldn't understand how this child—who would constantly rebuff me in public—had learned to be so chivalrous. It didn't make sense. Curt and I had always tried to teach our children good manners, but this was a bit extreme. Finally, I learned that it was because of William.

In kindergarten, Grant palled around with a child named William who had spinal muscular atrophy (SMA) and had been in a wheelchair since the age of one. According to his teacher, Grant insisted upon carrying William's bag and opening doors at school for William and his wheelchair. That practice had carried over to me.

One day I overheard Grant talking to his aunt Allison while we were dropping him off at school. He pointed at William and told her, "Aunt Allison, that's my best friend, William. God made him not to walk.'" After Grant got out of the car, Allison was choked up just talking about Grant's statement.

These moments, as wonderful as they are in retrospect, were the moments that confused me the most as a parent who was trying to understand her child. Before I knew about Asperger's, before I knew exactly what it was that made Grant different, the thing I kept coming back to was that he seemed like one big youthful, energetic contradiction. He would do something that would make you angry, and in the same breath he would tell you he loved you. This tendency made me refer to Grant as a child who would pinch you while he was hugging you.

School was a perfect example of this. He would struggle listening to adults, and he would fight us every step of the way as we tried to convince him to be more respectful, but then he'd turn around and display a thoughtfulness and a caring that no one else his age was able to. Yet for some reason, one never seemed to carry over to the other. He just never knew when to say when, and that obliviousness shifted the behavior from good to bad.

For years before Grant was diagnosed, this never-ending sea of contradictions was a constant source of confusion. The contradictions are what make you think this is just a phase, that somehow the "bad" part or the "odd" part of the contradiction will one day just stop, leaving only the "good" part behind. Isn't it funny how willing we are to assume that bad behavior is somehow different, but good behavior is normal? When I think back to what things were like before I knew about Asperger's, my mind goes to those parking lots and airports where I almost lost it. The tears and the screaming, the nights when I couldn't sleep because of what he'd done in school that day, or what I worried he might do the next. I also think about how often Grant would do something good, something that other kids just didn't do. The times when he would say a word or a phrase that would show a level of understanding and complexity that exceeded what I myself thought.

In those moments, I was always caught speechless, trying to understand how the same child who just uttered those words could have had a meltdown in the grocery store over pork chops two nights before. It didn't make sense.

The only answer I could come up with was that this was just who my child was, and I had better get used to it.

HAVING GIVEN UP ON trying to change his behavior, I resorted to giving in. Out of sheer frustration, I often compensated for Grant's issues in ways that favored him over the other kids. If we were somewhere and Grant started to scream about something, like choosing the movie to be played in the car, I didn't care whose turn it was to pick the movie—it was now Grant's turn. Eventually it was always Grant's turn. Whatever it took to keep him calm and quiet, I went with.

I had spent too many days negotiating with a four-year-old to get him to eat, get dressed, get in the car—you name it. Naturally, the other kids began to resent all the times Grant got his way. They ran out of patience with him, and how could I blame them? *I* was out of patience, too.

Grant and Gehrig butted heads the most. When Grant was in the first grade, he told his teachers that his brother didn't love him. You can imagine our embarrassment when we heard that. It sounded so terrible. We scolded Gehrig that night.

"Your brother thinks you don't love him," we said. "How does that make you feel?" In Gehrig's defense, he didn't know—none of us knew then—that Grant didn't have a way to filter sarcasm the way everyone else can. Normal kids joke around or they say things casually that sound like fighting words but aren't. Grant could only take things literally, but no one had any idea that that was the case.

That phone call from Grant's teacher got Curt and me to pay more attention to how the other kids were treating Grant. We noticed that the two older kids fought for Garrison's attention rather than Grant's because Garrison was cool and easy to be around.

The more I paid attention, the more I noticed that everyone yelled at Grant. A lot. Everyone was frustrated with him and didn't know what to do other than yell. Curt would come home from being on the road, and he'd yell at Grant. More than anyone's yelling, Curt's was like nails on a chalkboard to me. I couldn't stand it.

In addition to the issues with his siblings, Grant had other, more practical issues, like not being able to tie his shoes. That year we taught him how three times. Oddly, each time we tried, by the next day, he could not remember. He would immediately feel frustrated if I asked him to try again, or even tried to suggest that he might want to practice. Because it would bring up so much frustration, we would wait months at a time before asking him to try once more. Fortunately for Grant, Velcro shoes were in.

While we resorted to getting those shoes for him, we were still puzzled and concerned about his inability to tie his shoes. It bugged me, especially since I had worked at Foot Locker all through college. I'd seen kids his age tying their own shoes. It was a big accomplishment they liked to show off. Why couldn't Grant do that?

I worried that the other kids would notice he wasn't wearing lace-up shoes. He never seemed to worry about it himself, even though I did. He did have some lace-ups, which he wore for sports. I'd have to tie them for him, and I'd double-knot them so that in the middle of a game, he wouldn't be faced with having to have his mom come tie his shoes.

After a while, I learned to go more with my gut in terms of knowing which situations I shouldn't push with Grant. He was not always predictable, and I learned to recognize the feeling that maybe a situation just wasn't right for him.

That year we visited our old neighbors the Bauers in Arizona, who had kids around the same age as ours. Susan, their mother, asked if Grant could spend the night with them. They had recently gotten a new pool and their kids were old enough that they didn't need a pool fence.

I tried to be polite about it. "I wish I could let him," I told her, "but without a pool fence, I'm just not certain Grant wouldn't get in. I don't feel comfortable about it."

"Oh, Shonda, don't worry about it," she assured me. "There's no way. Do you really think he'd go in if we told him not to?"

We were standing in the house, looking out at the pool. The kids were done with swimming, and on to snacks. No sooner did my friend finish assuring me there would be no problem than Grant ran over and jumped into the pool. One of the earliest lessons that we taught him around the pool was that he should never go in if there were no adults around. But no matter how many times we tried to instill this in Grant, he didn't learn. His jumping in by himself that afternoon confirmed my fear.

"Grant, get out of the pool!" I yelled. Over and over I told him, *"You should know better!"* But he couldn't seem to understand what the problem was. He knew how to swim, and he figured that was all that mattered. He couldn't process that he could hit his head and no one would see. He couldn't process that there were rules and he was simply ignoring them.

I collected incidents like that. They were moments that left me uneasy about leaving Grant with other grown-ups. There were very few people I would let him go with. I said no to some people I actually think are great parents. But no matter how good they were, I never wanted them to have to be two thoughts ahead of Grant—and I couldn't trust that they would be.

A funny story about those neighbors: One day Susan and I were at the fence talking. Grant walked right past us and went into her house. He came back eating a Pop-Tart.

"What did you just do?" I asked. I was mortified that he was helping himself to their food.

"I just got a Pop-Tart," he said, not getting what was wrong with that.

"Why did you get it from their house?" I asked.

"Because they have better Pop-Tarts," he answered.

As strange as that logic was, it was the kind of logic he operated on, and no matter what we did, getting him to listen was an uphill battle.

Of all those battles, bedtime was the worst. There was no keeping Grant down and in bed all night. With my other kids, I'd put them to sleep, and occasionally they'd wake up asking for water, needing to go to the bathroom, or frightened from a nightmare. Grant, on the other hand, would get out of bed fifteen times at bedtime, almost without fail. It seemed as if he had to jump on that last nerve of mine just before bed. He would try to negotiate with me every night about going to bed. He wanted to stay up and play with his Legos, read some more, watch TV—anything but go to sleep. Curt played a made-up game called "Thumb Wars" with Grant each night at bedtime, which was basically just thumb wrestling. If Curt didn't, or they forgot, it was not odd at all for Grant to stroll into our bedroom at 3 A.M. and wake us up. Curt would yell, *"Grant, what the hell are you doing?"* In a very calm voice, Grant would reply, "You forgot Thumb Wars, Dad."

I discussed this with a friend whose kids were difficult around bedtime, too.

"I put locks on their doors that can only be opened from the outside," she said. "At first they might be very upset about it, but then they get used to it."

I have to admit, it felt a little extreme. But I was desperate. The boy simply would not stay in his bed. So I put a hook and latch on the outside of Grant's door.

The first week, he cried, screamed, and banged on the door every night. I found it impossible to ignore, and the guilt was just overwhelming. Sometimes I would find myself sitting outside his door until I knew he was asleep, so I could unlatch it. Having a lock there unnerved me—what if something were seriously wrong with him and he couldn't get out? What if there were a fire and Grant couldn't get out and I didn't have time to get to him?

While eventually Grant got sort of used to it, now *I* couldn't sleep. As long as that latch was down, I couldn't go to bed. After a couple of weeks, I decided I needed to find another way. What that would be, I had no idea.

While the sleeping situation was awful, the most heartbreaking thing I noticed about Grant was that if he got hurt, there was no way I could console him. He wouldn't let me—or anyone—so much as touch him. I couldn't pick him up and hug him, which is what you instinctively do as a parent when your child is hurt. It was that way from the time Grant was really small—maybe two years old—and continues to this day.

I remember one time shortly after we moved to Boston, Grant was playing outside with Gehrig. I had been trying to help those two bond, and it hadn't been easy. Grant badly wanted to have a relationship with his older brother, but they didn't seem to mix well (and still struggle at it today). That afternoon, when Grant was four or five and Gehrig was nine or ten, they got into a fight in the yard. They had been wrestling and they swung at each other. Grant came running inside, screaming and crying.

"Come here," I said. "Let me hold you." And I reached for him. But as soon as I did, he screamed louder.

"No!" he yelled. *"No! No!"*

I kept trying to get near him, but he kept pulling away and screaming. Finally I gave up.

"Fine," I told him. "I'll leave you alone." I didn't know what else to do at that point other than walk away, so I did.

"Mom!" he then cried. *"Mom!"* He didn't seem to like that I was walking away, either. I couldn't win.

"What do you want me to do?" I asked, completely frustrated. "Just tell me what you want me to do!"

"You didn't do *anything*!" he wailed. *"I was hurt and you didn't help me!"*

I was at a complete loss about how to help him. I couldn't hold him, I couldn't talk him down. I came to the conclusion that I just had to let him lie there on the floor and work it out for himself.

"Mom, how could you not do anything?!" he continued. *"You didn't even help me!"*

I was on the verge of tears. I didn't have an answer. I searched but couldn't find one. I felt like a failure as a mother. This was motherhood

101: You see your kid fall and you go to pick him up, but you can't pick him up, you can't stop him from crying, and you can't make him feel loved. Catch 22: And then he blames you for not making him feel loved.

I called my mother. "Mom, how can I be a mother to him if he doesn't let me hold him?" I begged, completely distraught. "He won't let me love him, and he won't love me back. How can you love someone who won't love you?"

My mom was speechless. Grant had managed to stump the master.

six
The Boy Who Cried Lice

✳

THE YEARS WENT BY AND BASEBALL CONTINUED. AS CURT GOT older, the ballpark consumed more of his time, which meant less time for me, less time for the kids, and less time for him to see with his own eyes how very different Grant was.

As Grant got older, his behavior became more worrisome. At a certain point, Garrison, who was three years younger, began to seem more mature in many ways than Grant did. He knew how to listen to adults and how to play well with other kids. He played the games kids his age were into, as opposed to Grant, who remained obsessed with things that most of the kids in his grade had moved on from years earlier.

In addition, there was a natural affinity between Curt and Garrison. Curt found Garrison easy to be with, and Garrison just adored Curt. When Curt would go on the road, Garrison would get sad—more so than any of the other kids had. He always wanted to know when Curt was coming home, a question that Grant almost never seemed to ask.

Specifics aside, much of Grant's behavior spoke for itself. He never seemed to connect with his older siblings, never could relate to them. This was not just because they were annoyed that I gave him his way. Grant pushed the definition of "annoying little brother" to new heights.

He would find the oddest ways to interact with all of us. For instance, he went through a phase where he liked to scare us. He'd come running around a corner and scream, and it would be utterly startling. We'd each get mad when he did that to us and scream at him. However, our being upset never seemed to register with him. It never got old to him. He would keep doing it, and his reaction was the same the twentieth time as it was the first. Meanwhile the rest of us were all left to wonder where we could find his "off" button.

He also went through a phase where he insisted on squirting water from a water bottle on other kids on his football team. At first the kids would laugh and seemed to enjoy it, but after the thirtieth time or so, the other kids had enough and would be screaming and yelling at Grant. He never understood that the joke had long been over.

Another phase Grant went through was shoving, tagging, and taunting people. The shoving seemed like a misguided attempt at being playful. It started at home, with Gehrig giving Grant playful little pushes that I didn't mind because they seemed like a form of social bonding between the two of them, who had always been like oil and water. It was sort of a kidding-around push, and it seemed affectionate. But Grant didn't get the subtleties of it. He didn't realize it was okay between his brother and him, but wouldn't be okay with kids he didn't know.

Sure enough, Grant started giving little shoves to kids at school and at his siblings' games. Some kids he knew and others he didn't. Then he started doing it to kids bigger than he was, not realizing the dangers of that. Naturally, the other kids didn't like it, but he never seemed to pick up on that and he persisted. I just kept hoping that at some point he'd get a clue just from being around and interacting with other kids.

There was no denying that Curt's absence made things a struggle. While baseball was the engine that our family was built on, it became increasingly difficult to cope with Grant's behavior on my own. When Curt was away, it always felt like a nonstop WWF match in my house. I'd call Curt most nights and tell him I was exhausted from dealing with Grant and the many ways he bothered us and other people. "Go to bed," Curt would say. If life were only that simple. To make matters worse, I was suffering from a deficit of adult conversation. I almost never got to talk to other grown-ups. On most days our phone call would be my only chance to talk and to unload. This created tension between us. I would go on about all the ways in which the kids were being difficult, but it would just make Curt feel frustrated because he couldn't do anything about it long distance.

GIVEN THIS HISTORY OF Grant's odd behavior and outbursts, it would be easy for people to assume that he was some kind of monster child. But he wasn't, I swear.

Grant was actually one of the sweetest, most loving kids you might ever come across. For a boy who doesn't read social cues, he is incredibly sensitive toward others, especially those in need. Grant doesn't pick up on facial expressions, but he can instantly identify those who are in need of compassion. He's not uncomfortable approaching the situation with that person, whereas most people would avoid the issue altogether. It's one of the things that has always made his challenging and odd behaviors forgivable—and for brief periods, even forgettable.

He has always been known for his affection. Back when he was in preschool his teachers said that what they most remembered about him was that he would hug everyone. He hugged the teachers hello, and if he came in and didn't see them, he would come look for them just to say hello. At the end of the first day that he rode on the school bus, the bus driver called me over.

"Grant did the sweetest thing," she told me. "He thanked me and then hugged me before getting off the bus."

My heart was warmed. The sad part for her was that while she loved it, there are rules forbidding the drivers from making physical contact with the children. "I hated having to have a conversation with him about this, telling him he couldn't hug me anymore," she said.

Unfortunately, in his sweetness, Grant would often cross social boundaries leading to all kinds of awkwardness. By the time he was in second grade he would still be trying to hold hands with the other boys in his class, something you did in preschool and kindergarten. He didn't understand why the kids would say, "Get off me." He was totally unaware that he was being ridiculed.

This obliviousness to ridicule was at once frustrating and remarkable. It could cause him to dominate a conversation with kids and interrupt them at every turn, but it also meant that he was completely genuine in his affection for those around him. What really distinguished him from the other kids was that when deciding who deserved his love and attention, he never stopped to consider how other people would view him.

Cooper, who is my brother's son and Grant's cousin, has many food allergies, and from early on Grant was always protective of him. When Cooper was around, Grant would constantly check ingredients on food we had in the home. "Hey," he'd shout out, "does this have peanuts in it? Because Cooper can't have it if it has peanuts." Our meals and snacktimes were overshadowed by Grant's desire to protect his cousin. His actions were more like those of an overly concerned parent. Yet Grant was just a child.

In first grade, Grant became best friends with a boy named Stephen who has Down syndrome. Grant just naturally gravitated toward him. He stood by Stephen and watched out for him. Their first grade teacher, Mrs. Callahan, was struck by this and mentioned it in our conference: "His sweetness and sensitivity toward accepting others, especially those with disabilities, is an admirable quality in someone so young," she said.

She shared a story with me about Grant: In class one afternoon when Stephen had finished his art project, Grant saw his picture. He then took it upon himself to show off the project to the other kids in the class, telling everyone how nice a job Stephen had done. His actions were those of a parent or teacher trying to boost self-confidence in a child. This behavior would have been advanced for a senior in college, much less a first-grader. Grant was teaching his classmates how to praise and encourage Stephen.

Mrs. Callahan told me another story about Grant that spoke volumes about how powerfully he felt sympathy in certain situations. "We were studying Columbus and learning how he had taken some Native Americans with him on one of his voyages back to Europe," she said. "We had a whole class discussion about how those Native Americans must have felt being taken away from their families and being forced to live in a place that was unfamiliar to them. Grant didn't say much during that discussion, but came to me later in the day and said, 'You know, Mrs. Callahan, I was thinking. If that was me without my family going to a new land, I would be crying so hard that my tears would sink the ship.' It was another one of those moments when I realized how sensitive and loving Grant is."

She said it was also a sign that he was a deep thinker who took time to process and digest information in order to make sense of it all. Not just that, but she also told me he could write poetry. At the time I thought, *What kind of poetry is a kid going to write in first grade?* But after I ran a marathon, he gave me a poem. It said, "Running is hard, jogging is, too. But you do it so fast, people thought you flew." Not bad for a little kid.

If his emotional depth was one thing that showed me Grant was not like other kids, another was his intelligence, which I was amazed by time and time again. While Grant's ability to get hyperfocused on things could be a problem when we were in the toy store, it also had an upside, especially when it carried over to his school life. He would get locked in on subjects—dinosaurs, for example—and have to learn everything there was to know about them. It would be all he'd talk about or think about. He'd want to read books on the subject, and I'd get him everything I could find. As a result, Grant was an incredibly smart kid who devoured books and information with a remarkable appetite. One teacher told me that Grant would get so hooked on a book, he'd read it nonstop, even walking and reading at the same time.

As if that weren't enough, Grant wouldn't just read. He'd speed-read. I discovered that talent one night when the kids were all reading before bed. I was putting everyone to sleep, and when I got to Grant's room, he had finished half the book.

"Stop messing around and read," I said.

"But I am," he answered.

"Bull," I responded, cutting him off. "There's no way you're already on that page."

We went back and forth a few times, and finally I decided to ask him a few questions about the book. He knew all the answers! I was shocked, especially because he couldn't read too fast out loud.

When Grant was in first or second grade, he was fixated on naked mole rats. He learned about them through the Disney show *Kim Possible*, which had one as a character. He became completely obsessed with these animals, talking about them all the time. The school librarian took notice and bought a book on the subject for Grant. He loved that book and read it over and over. It was so sweet of her.

Sadly, that thoughtful librarian passed away from cancer during summer break. The school advised parents to tell their kids before school resumed in the fall. We didn't know what to expect when we told Grant, but we weren't prepared for what we saw. As we said the words, he hesitated for a minute and then slowly his entire body just deflated. He was heartbroken, and he cried for a good twenty minutes. It was a deep, heartfelt cry, one that left little doubt about how affected he was. Though he did not see this woman every day, she was an integral part of his experience at school. He was simply devastated.

As a mother, I found this tough to watch, but it also revealed how powerfully sympathetic he was. I was astounded by how caring he could be. Though there were times when Curt and I questioned his respect for us as parents, he seemed to have a respect for life that went far beyond anything I'd encountered in other kids.

———◆———

I SHOULD REALLY GO BACK and check my horoscope for 2007. So much was happening to my family then, and the chaos hit such a fever pitch, there were moments when I wondered whether I was under some kind of hex.

Early that year, both the good and the bad aspects of Grant's behavior began to pile up in my mind. While I still didn't know that anything was wrong clinically, I couldn't shake the idea of how different from other kids—both our own and those we knew—he was proving himself to be.

Part of the problem was that despite my instincts that something was wrong, I felt as if people second-guessed me whenever I brought up Grant's behavior. When I would talk to friends and family about how Grant acted, there was always an excuse, something that they felt made the behavior somehow my fault. They weren't necessarily trying to point the finger at me, and everyone was well-intentioned about giving advice, but all their ideas seemed to place the blame squarely on me, especially because Curt was on the road so often.

Grant didn't respect me.

I spoiled him.

I wasn't firm enough.

No matter whom I spoke to about the trends I saw in Grant, everyone seemed to dismiss it with a wave of the hand and an overly simplified generalization. None of it felt right.

And then there were the times when it wasn't just friends and family who were questioning my instincts but my own husband. This was usually because Curt wasn't around enough to know what I was talking about—he hadn't witnessed certain behaviors in Grant firsthand. Other times, he seemed to think I was latching on to an excuse for not having control. Every night when he wasn't home, I'd give him the play-by-play on how Grant had acted, and often he'd find a way to retrain the lens onto something else that didn't involve Grant. Curt still wasn't that close with Grant, and each night I reached out in the hope that I could draw them together. Yet something in my communication with Curt was being lost in translation; I didn't know what I could do to make him see what I was going through.

Curt was also skeptical about the way behavioral illnesses like ADHD were becoming excuses for modern children being disrespectful to their parents. Though Curt himself had been accurately diagnosed with ADHD many years before, and took Adderall to deal with it, he still felt that ADHD was diagnosed too frequently in kids. I, too, had been wary of this suddenly common diagnosis, and I was against medicating kids so casually for it.

But then, in early 2007, as I was starting to think more about Grant's behavior, I began to notice things about Gehrig as well. He was struggling much more in middle school than he had earlier, which is certainly not abnormal, but for someone so bright, it made no sense. His grades didn't reflect how intelligent he was. It seemed that over the past couple of years a cycle would repeat itself—he'd find himself far behind and depressed about catching up, and I couldn't get him to focus or spend nearly enough time on homework. He had a tutor come work with him twice a week, and I was able to check his homework online, but still he would spend more time trying to get out of doing his homework than actually doing it.

At the time, Curt was getting ready to leave for spring training, so I couldn't rely on him to help me stay on top of Gehrig and his schoolwork. Gehrig and I would go through the same cycle over and over again: I would exhaust myself chasing him into the dining room, where he was supposed to be working. But as soon as I'd leave the room, he'd wander into another room to do something, anything, besides his homework. He'd go watch television in the den, follow one of the dogs outside to play with it, go into the computer room to e-mail his friends, or worse, to agitate his siblings.

When report cards came out, Gehrig was shocked and sad. After many years as an average student, his grades now reflected that he was below average. He broke into tears right in front of us, but knowing how hard it had been to get him to focus on work, Curt and I were angry with him. We fell back on the approach we always used back then: punishment. We tried to figure out what we could take away from him for a while to show that we were serious and to persuade him to do better. But it's hard to take something away from a kid who doesn't treasure anything enough to be worried about losing it—unlike his sister, who would view being docked a sleepover as capital punishment. Gehrig also didn't have as many friends as he used to. Although he was well liked at school, he didn't put much effort into socializing after school and on the weekends.

After watching Gehrig struggle with this for a while, I was tired of the fights and concerned about how much he dreaded homework every night. I went online and realized he fit every single symptom on the list for ADHD. Not a few—every one. (What did we do before the Internet?) I printed out one of the lists I found and brought it to Curt in his home office.

"Look at this," I said, handing the paper to him. Curt glanced over the list of symptoms: not being able to sit still, not being able to concentrate, doing poorly in school despite evidence of high intelligence, difficulty committing to plans and therefore forming close friendships. Curt looked up at me blankly.

"This is Gehrig to a tee," I insisted. It seemed so obvious to me. But one look at Curt and I knew this would be a battle.

"He just needs more discipline and structure," he argued. Curt didn't want to buy into the ADHD idea. He assumed that since Gehrig acted very much the way he had acted when he was a teenage boy, Gehrig was lazy or just acting like a boy. Here was Curt, who has ADHD and has been medicated for most of his adult life, not seeing the irony and the parallels between himself and his son. He was missing it completely. I could barely contain my frustration. I spent all my time parenting virtually by myself while trying to discipline Gehrig and the others and instill structure. My life as a parent was based on structure. I knew that wasn't the problem. It wasn't a matter of intelligence, and it wasn't a matter of discipline.

"Well, I'm going to have Gehrig tested," I said, and I made the appointment with the neurologist. Sure enough, the test results came back positive. Now Gehrig needed medication, but I was worried about medicating him. I grew up avoiding medication except when it was desperately needed. But my attempts at getting Gehrig to focus weren't working. I wanted to help him become the student that I knew he could be. I filled the prescription and he began to take the medication.

My biggest mistake in this was not discussing it with Curt. I didn't want to fight with him about it, especially after he had given me so much pushback when I'd merely suggested that Gehrig had ADHD. This was pretty much in keeping with our tendency to avoid talking about certain difficult topics. While we were always very open and honest with each other, our lives intersected infrequently because of his baseball schedule. Our time together, and that with our family, was so rare and valuable that many times we'd both table an item we knew would produce conflict. It was one of the unfortunate and unintended consequences of our baseball lives, but we acted that way out of a desire to maximize what little time we had together.

So when the 2007 season started and Curt was too busy to notice, I started Gehrig on Adderall. From day one he had issues with the medication. He didn't like the way the pills made him feel. Even though he was more focused, he complained of a funny taste in his mouth. He said it also altered his personality and made it so he wasn't hungry.

"I don't want to take this stuff, Mom," he said.

"I'm sorry, honey," I told him, "but this is important for you. It will help you do better in school, and in life."

"*Please* can I stop?" he begged.

"Absolutely not," I said.

Pretty soon, Gehrig decided on his own to stop taking the Adderall. He began by burying the medicine in the soil beneath our houseplants or in the trash. Sometimes he'd just leave it on the counter. I thought he was taking it, but in fact, he wasn't.

Since he'd only been on the medication the last six weeks of school that year, it was difficult to gauge whether it had worked for him. After that, I stopped filling his prescriptions. I wasn't going to waste the money, or the medicine. I never gave him medication on the weekends, and there seemed to be no reason to give it to him in the summer.

Although it was hard to discern whether the diagnosis was having any immediate impact, Gehrig's testing positive for ADHD gave me more confidence in my parental judgment. I had trusted my instincts that there was something wrong with him and I had been right. The only problem was that now I was starting to see some of the same behaviors that led me to be concerned about Gehrig in Gabby and Grant as well.

As it turned out, I wasn't the only one. In May, just a few months after Gehrig was diagnosed with ADHD, administrators in our school system let me know that, like Gehrig (and like their dad), both Gabby and Grant seemed to have problems focusing. They thought the two should be tested for ADHD, so I made two appointments with a neurologist for the middle of the summer. (By the way, I went back and checked my horoscope from 2007; it said to buy stock in the company that produces Adderall.)

THAT SUMMER OF 2007, when Grant was seven, I enrolled him in day camp. This was the first time I let Grant do something on his own outside school.

It was not a decision I took lightly. I knew full well that I had avoided sending him on his own to anything nonschool-related for years and that certain elements of his behavior might make this a bit hard. Gabby went to the same camp, which made me feel a little more comfortable, but still I wasn't sure. I went back and forth thinking about it for weeks, but in the end I decided that at some point I would have to let him do things most kids enjoy. Summer camp is practically a right of passage where we live, and I convinced myself he was mature enough for summer day camp.

I was wrong.

Every day Gabby would come home with horror stories about the ways Grant had misbehaved that day. Angry and embarrassed, she would tell me how all the kids would be called from the pool to move on to the next activity, and after they all exited the pool, Grant would jump right back in the water. To most people, this would seem to be an obvious lack of respect for the camp counselors. Gabby was routinely uncomfortable with his actions, and I can't even imagine what labels he was given by the other kids and the counselors that summer.

When I'd go to pick him up at the end of the day, I'd try to ask him about the things Gabby had reported, but he didn't seem to have any idea what I was talking about. Sometimes I'd try to make a little joke out of it and say, "I hope you didn't have too rough a day, Grant," but he wouldn't say much or anything at all.

In the mornings I would try to prep him, saying things like "Grant, you need to listen to the adults at camp, okay? That's really important." Or I'd tell him, "If you want to have friends, you've got to get along with people and follow directions." But no matter what I said to him, Gabby would come home with a list of things Grant had done wrong or ways he'd gotten on people's nerves.

In the middle of all this, Grant told his counselors that he had lice. When his hair grew to a certain length, it annoyed him, so he would constantly scratch his head. One day when he was scratching, his counselor asked him about it.

"Grant, are you okay?" he asked.

"Uh, my sister had lice," he explained. "So I probably have them now."

What Grant failed to mention in relaying this news was that Gabby had had lice at the beginning of the previous school year. She'd been clear for months. Of course, the camp called me right away, and I had to go get him. I explained to them that his sister's case of lice had been close to a year before, but still they made me take him home. I showed up the next day with this kid who had hardly any hair on his head—I'd given him a very short cut so that it would be a long time before it grew back and he started scratching his head again.

They let Grant back into camp, but it didn't really matter. After about two weeks of hearing Gabby's upsetting reports about Grant's behavior at camp, I decided to take him out. It wasn't working. Instead, I decided to introduce him to football.

Among Grant's more troubling behaviors was his penchant for running and slamming into people—mostly me. I became Grant's security blanket at an early age, and for some reason he liked to run toward me and bang his body against mine. As he got bigger, it became harder to take. It started to really hurt! Yet nothing I would do or say could stop him.

It was his habit of body-slamming me that made me think Grant would like football. Since he wasn't going to camp anymore and I needed to find something for him to do. I enrolled him in Pop Warner football, a very regimented program. I thought, *Grant is going to love this.* Curt and I both thought this would be the answer to his behavioral issues because it was really strict—bordering on military-level strict.

Because he was so young, I went to the practices, held in the early evenings, where there were lots of other parents, too. Pop Warner is very parent-oriented. I had high hopes for Grant and Pop Warner football—it's a really great program. But right from the first week, there was trouble. It wasn't long before all the coaches—there were about seven of them—knew Grant's name.

Someone was always yelling, *"Grant!"* He was always going the wrong way or not paying attention so he didn't know to go where he was told. Then I started to join in. I was torn between sitting there silently, letting his coaches try to get his respect, and yelling *"Grant!"* myself to try and help them control him. Sometimes I felt like I was causing even more of a scene.

There was one coach in particular who wasn't having any of Grant's behavior. I swear he dragged Grant everywhere by the helmet. He would grab him by the face mask and pull him. On the one hand, I totally understood how that coach felt. How else was he going to get Grant to go where he was supposed to? There was no getting through to him. On the other hand, the coach's solution seemed pretty harsh, and it upset me. I didn't know what to do with myself.

The whole thing was baffling to me. I sat there watching everyone else's kids, who were tough and eager to learn. Meanwhile, Grant had to be dragged around by his coaches. And there would be plays where he would get knocked down and then just lie there in the middle of the field.

Now and then, Grant would parlay his love of body-slamming into knocking someone else down. Because they determined teams by weight rather than age, Grant, who was a bit bulky for a second-grader, was in with some kids who were older than he was. During one of the practices, he went in there and started running. Well, he ran right into this fourth-grader and knocked him to the ground. Hard. My jaw dropped. I wondered whether the kid was going to get up and clock him.

Suddenly Grant stood up and turned around to all the parents, put both his arms up, and shouted, "I knocked over a fourth-grader!"

It was hilarious, and all the parents seemed to laugh, too. Of course, two plays later he was lying on the ground himself, and just sitting there. You never knew when he was going to be on, and it was rare when he was.

During each practice, I would talk on the phone to Curt, who was usually at the Red Sox clubhouse getting ready for a game.

"I don't think this is a good idea," I told him over and over. "For some reason, this isn't working."

"No, this is *exactly* what he needs," Curt said. Of course, Curt wasn't sitting there for two hours every night just praying that this night was going to be easier than the last one.

I kept taking Grant to Pop Warner football, but things didn't get any better. As they moved into working on specific football plays, Grant wouldn't follow directions. He wouldn't listen, and he wouldn't look where he needed to, especially if someone was trying to make eye contact with him.

So there we were, night after night. More and more often, Grant would get knocked down and then not move from the field. I started to notice that the other parents were getting frustrated. The coaches were finding it very difficult to keep him focused during the games. While he was there, he'd do annoying things like throw his helmet or squirt the other kids with water or, always inappropriately, try to be funny. The kids didn't think it was funny, and neither did the parents, who took Pop Warner football very seriously.

I thought I had a solution: I'd get Curt involved with Grant.

"Curt, go throw a football with Grant," I suggested. "Maybe if you show some interest, it'll start to click for him." I also hoped this would help the two of them connect. I hoped that maybe football would become their thing together.

So one afternoon when Curt was back home for a few days, he went outside with Grant and the football. And I swear, Curt was not out there ten minutes before he walked back in, looking really frustrated.

"He's not processing anything," Curt said.

"What do you mean, 'He's not processing anything'?" I yelled. I was annoyed at Curt for coming right back in. I felt like he hadn't given it enough effort, and I didn't understand how he could so quickly throw up his hands.

"I mean that he's not processing anything that I'm saying," Curt explained. "He's not getting any of it."

There was something about what he said—the word *processing,* in particular—it seemed to make sense. Grant couldn't process social cues, he couldn't process when the joke was over, he clearly couldn't process facial expressions, he didn't process instructions by camp counselors or other figures of authority, he didn't process what was socially acceptable and what was not. I instantly went over to the computer and started Googling.

I put in the words *not processing information,* and all these links came up about autism. But that made no sense to me. I knew kids with autism, and Grant didn't seem autistic. Before I knew it, I'd been reading online for an hour, and I wasn't sure what it meant.

Fortunately, back in May, I'd made that appointment for Grant to see a neurologist because his school thought he might have ADHD. Judging from some aspects of Grant's behavior, ADHD seemed like a logical diagnosis. He never sat still. He was more hyperactive and easily distracted than any of the others. As a friend once said to me, "Did you ever notice that Grant doesn't walk into any room? He runs, jumps, hops, and swings from lamps before slamming into you to stop." If that didn't seem to fit the bill for ADHD, then I didn't know what would.

The appointment was one week away. I used that time to brace myself to ask the doctor a question I wasn't sure I wanted the answer to: Could Grant be autistic?

seven

The Missing Piece

✳

BEFORE THE WORD AUTISM POPPED UP ON THE SCREEN, I'D ALREADY skipped the formal diagnosis and gone straight to what my heart and my head were telling me: Grant had ADHD. ADHD just seemed to be in the air in our house.

All that changed after I typed the words *not processing information* into Google. Let me tell you, a little bit of information about something like autism can be a bad thing. And all the things people write online about their horrible experiences can be very dangerous to a nervous mother who's trying to figure out how to do the right thing for her son.

In truth, I had begun to doubt my unprofessional ADHD diagnosis for Grant three weeks prior to the appointment with the neurologist, when he had to undergo three hours of testing—written and verbal tests. After the three hours were up, Grant came out of the office with the woman who had administered the tests. She looked as if she'd just gone fifteen rounds with Muhammad Ali.

"Grant tried to negotiate every single thing that I asked him to do," she said.

"Everything?" I asked, cringing.

"Every single thing," she replied in a trying-to-be-nice voice, but clearly exhausted. "He'd say, 'I will only read this paragraph if I can lay on the couch with my feet up in the air.' He fought me on every request. This is by far the hardest I have had to work to get these tests completed with any patient."

The day of the neurologist's appointment, Curt was away, so I had to take Grant on my own. My father came along to drive me, because I'd had foot surgery and wasn't healing well. (I think that may have been God's way of protecting me: not letting me be alone, making sure I had moral support.)

The neurologist, Dr. Rosenberger, brought me, alone, into his office. The first piece of news was no surprise at all: Grant did in fact have ADHD. The doctor would prescribe Adderall. But there was more.

"Grant is on the autistic spectrum," he said. He then drew a scale for me that showed low-functioning autism at one end and high-functioning at the other. "Grant is at the high-functioning end of this."

I was looking at this thing, and hearing the doctor talk, but not really. I suddenly felt like I was in a tunnel, and I just kept thinking to myself, *Try to focus and process what he's saying.* I was having a hard time, though. The word *autism* had not really been in my vocabulary. It was always something other parents' children had, and I had been hoping against hope that all my Googling had brought up the wrong results. But now there was this doctor in front of me saying my son had it, which made this all too real. Even though it made so much sense, I did not want to hear what the doctor was saying. Tears started pouring from my eyes before I could realize that I was crying.

When I stepped out of the doctor's office and met Grant and my dad in the waiting room, it was very obvious that I had been crying. I stopped for a few minutes, but then the tears were streaming again. Grant reached for my hand and held it, trying to comfort me. I didn't say anything to him about what had just happened. He was seven years old. What was I going to tell him? How was it that I was just learning my seven-year-old child was autistic? Wasn't that something I should have known, or been told, years ago? In an odd way, you'd think I would want to just hug him, yet I actually felt the opposite. I couldn't hug. My arms suddenly felt like I couldn't lift them. I just kept turning over the same words in my head: How am I going to tell him?

And then how was I going to tell Curt? Of course, he wasn't just off at an office somewhere, he was on the road pitching for the Red Sox. I couldn't think. I was completely numb. I couldn't really communicate. Everything was changing in that moment, and in the moments when I became fully conscious, my heart was heavy and aching. It was the biggest heartache I had ever felt in my life.

When I got home, I told the babysitter and I told my mother. And I cried every time I said the word *autism*. I didn't call Curt. I couldn't tell him on the phone. I needed to tell him in person. I needed to see the reaction on his face. I'd see him that night. Every year I made a trip with one of the kids to see their dad at an away game, and it just so happened that this annual trip would be tonight. This time it was Garrison's turn. Once I got there, I'd tell Curt.

In the hours before I saw him, I was nervous about telling him what I'd learned from the neurologist. Part of me suspected that he wouldn't believe it—he'd think the diagnosis was wrong. In the past, when I'd talked about aspects of Grant's behavior, Curt either didn't see it or didn't understand it.

When we got to the hotel, Curt took one look at me and knew something was up.

"I can tell something is wrong," he said. "What is it?"

"I need to talk to you," I said.

"Tell me," he begged.

I took a deep breath and looked Curt in the eye. "Grant has autism spectrum disorder," I said.

Curt looked at me and nodded his head. Then he said, "That makes so much sense."

I couldn't believe how easy that was. It seemed too easy. My feelings were mixed. I was relieved that Curt got it, that he didn't argue with me. I couldn't have argued with him then, I was too emotionally raw. But it also felt anticlimactic. Here I had been on this three-year journey of discovering Grant's differences since he was about four, and it had been this huge struggle, a struggle I'd been fighting with Curt about, trying to get him to see. And then all I had to do was say the words, tell him what the neurologist said, and like that, he accepted it. In a way I felt angry that Curt hadn't gone through everything I had to get to that place of knowing and understanding, that I'd had to do it all on my own.

While telling Curt did bring a huge wave of relief, it also cleared the way for me to go to a new well of anxiety, a place where, because I didn't know much about autism, I began to envision all the horrible futures Grant might have in store for him. What would it mean for him as he got older? Would he be able to function and socialize? Would he make friends? My mind irrationally moved from one tragic image to the next as I focused on what Grant wouldn't be and what he had lost. I pictured him with no friends, not being able to get along in the world or hold a job someday. I pictured him totally alone.

"We'll get through this, Shonda," Curt said as he held me. "We can get through anything."

We'd made a pact when we first got married: No matter how bad things ever got, neither one of us could leave. We'd need each other to get through this.

When the tears subsided they were replaced with visions of the past, visions I had to come to terms with. Every time I'd run out of patience with Grant, all the yelling, the punishing, the feelings of frustration, the anger—he'd endured all of this, although he'd never done anything intentionally to deserve it. He wasn't ignoring me when I yelled; he just wasn't processing what I'd said. So from sadness I shifted into guilt. It's the guilt that all parents feel no matter what their kids are like, only magnified through the lens of this diagnosis that gave shape and definition to his actions. Suddenly his behavior was explainable, while mine was not. How confused Grant must have been. How lost. How could I, his mother, the person who was supposed to love him above all else, have failed him so completely?

Sitting there with Curt, turning over the last seven years of my life, I was struck by the overwhelming and profound realization that every parent has had at one time or another: There is no such thing as a perfect child. Growing up, imagining my life as a mother, of course I envisioned my children as perfect. My mother had me walk a chalk line. I was taught by the best. Then, when I met Curt, it raised the bar even higher. Some people might not expect genius from a baseball player, but Curt is a very intelligent and well-read man, a serious bookworm who plows through volume after volume of history, especially of World War II. He's also a total computer geek and into complicated board games that I can't even begin to understand. So not only did I imagine that our kids would be natural athletes; they'd also be brilliant.

And yet despite my visions of perfection, I was shocked to learn that while my kids were all great in their own ways, not one of them was a star student or a serious athlete, which could be awkward when they showed up on a playing field and the other parents expected them to be outstanding because of their last name.

Though it's one thing to make peace with your kids not being academically or athletically exceptional and realize how they are each special in their own ways, it's another thing entirely to come to terms with one of your children being significantly different. This is every parent's worst nightmare, that their child will be labeled different in some way, whether it's a physical disability, social awkwardness, or coming from the wrong side of the tracks. The child who is different stands out and faces huge social and emotional consequences. The other kids notice who is different. Just the word *different* seems to be a bad thing, carrying all sorts of assumptions and stigmas.

Different means hardship, *different* means struggle. It may seem like a reductive way of looking at the world, but as pretty much any parent will tell you, children can be incredibly cruel, and nothing attracts that cruelty like a kid who is labeled *different*.

As I turned over the word *different* in my head, I found myself thinking of junior high. Throughout my elementary years, I had been in school with only kids from my neighborhood, Dundalk. Nobody in Dundalk had a lot. We all got by, but nobody was anywhere near well off. Then, in junior high, we were put together with kids from all over the area in a school outside our neighborhood. This new diversity meant that there were now kids with more money. I lived in a row house, and they lived in individual houses. I was made very aware of that difference, among others.

It didn't have an impact on me, though, until a big student council event I took part in during seventh grade. I dressed up for our big district meeting. Since I didn't have anything too special to wear in my own closet, I borrowed some clothes from my mom. I felt very put-together when I left the house that morning, and I couldn't wait to get to school and go to that meeting.

When I got there, though, I encountered a group of wealthier girls, gathered together and wearing the latest designer jeans.

"Her pants are too short," I heard one girl whisper to another in a pack of about five of them. They all giggled as they gave me the once-over.

"And what kind of outfit is that?" another asked, just loud enough for me to hear.

I was devastated. Completely humiliated. I spent most of the rest of the day hiding in the bathroom, except for when I knew I was needed in the meetings. I cried and cried. I felt like an outcast. The day seemed to take forever to end.

After feeling the way I did that day, I was determined never to let any child of mine feel that way or treat anyone that way. While Gehrig and Gabby had ADHD, I didn't worry too much about them being stigmatized for it, since there are so many kids who struggle with that. But now that Grant had autism, how was he going to get along? How was he going to avoid being labeled as different? Ever since I'd been a parent, I'd been raising my kids so that they wouldn't have to know the pain of being different. I'd been confident that my parenting skills were enough to get them through whatever obstacles they faced. Now, with this diagnosis, suddenly I wasn't so sure. All I could think of was myself in the seventh grade, sitting in the bathroom stall at school, waiting for the school day to end, and how I never wanted Grant to feel the way I had.

SCHOOL STARTED TWO WEEKS later. We had yet to receive all the details from Grant's tests at the neurologist's office, so we'd made another appointment for both Curt and me to go a few weeks into the school year. One day before our follow-up appointment with the doctor, I was at Grant's school when I bumped into a school administrator in the parking lot.

"So Grant has Asperger's syndrome, right?" she asked.

"Asperger's syndrome?" I replied. I had heard the term before, but I didn't really know what it meant. "No, the neurologist didn't say that to me." I suddenly felt panicked. "He said something about Grant being on the autism spectrum, but we're going for another meeting soon."

I was frazzled. Was this another thing I needed to look up online and learn about? I tried to keep myself together and resisted the urge to run to the computer. All that had gotten me last time was worried. With our appointment close enough, I figured I could wait and find out for sure what was going on.

When the date finally rolled around, I was relieved that Curt was there to come with me. Now he, too, could hear this straight from the doctor. In addition to giving us more details about Grant's situation, the doctor also confirmed what the school administrator had said: Grant had Asperger's syndrome. I asked the doctor to explain it to us so that Curt and I could both hear it.

The doctor explained that Asperger's is the result of different wiring in the brain's frontal lobe. It makes certain things—especially social cues and interactions—very challenging for kids who suffer from it. Yet they are some of the most empathetic, loving, and intelligent people in the world. They tend to be very bright, too. Albert Einstein, Benjamin Franklin, George Washington, Napoleon, Abraham Lincoln, and Harry Truman are all believed to have had Asperger's. He told us there are also sensory issues—explaining why Grant needs to touch things, and also why he likes to slam himself into people. There are problems with certain kinds of processing, especially when tasks require multiple steps. And transitions can be difficult. We knew that last part all too well, considering how hard it had always been to get Grant from point A to point B, even if ice cream or Legos were at point B.

One of the most surprising things the doctor said was that we shouldn't write this information in Grant's school file. That made no sense to me. He didn't think we should put a label on him. I didn't know how he would get help with his problems at school if his school didn't know he had Asperger's. I wanted to tell them, not only because they could help him, but selfishly, as well: I needed them to know that the challenging aspects of Grant's personality were not the result of bad parenting on my part. I'm not sure why this was so important to me, but it was.

The most eye-opening thing the neurologist pointed out was that Grant wasn't acting out or being difficult on purpose. He acted the way he did because of the way his brain was wired. He couldn't help himself, and our yelling at him was not only unhelpful, it was making matters worse. In his world, in his brain, his actions, reactions, and outbursts were perfectly normal. They were all he knew how to do.

Suddenly my mind flipped through a slideshow of every time I'd lost my patience with Grant and screamed at him. I felt awful. Grant had never meant to be mean. He'd never intended to be disrespectful. He did all the things he did because his brain told him to. In response, we'd yelled and yelled at him. That was going to have to stop. Our yelling days were over.

Toward the end of the meeting, the doctor switched gears. "Shonda," he said, "I think you should consider getting some help."

I was stunned. "What do you mean, 'help'?" I snapped.

"Maybe some medication, maybe talk to someone."

I felt a flame rush up through me. It was the heat of anger. I was mortified. Who was this guy to tell me I needed help? In front of Curt? I felt as if he was criticizing me, saying, "Oh, Curt, you're fine, but your wife? She's totally nuts!" I had been pushing myself day after day for years, juggling a family that had three kids with ADHD, one of whom apparently had Asperger's—not to mention a husband who also had ADHD and was never around. And now this professional was telling me I wasn't doing a very good job of it. I could barely contain myself.

"I beg your pardon?" I said, my voice bristling with annoyance.

"I just mean that you have so much on your plate. This might be easier for you to handle if you had something or someone to help you emotionally."

Maybe the timing was off. I had just finished taking in all this information about Grant. I wasn't ready for this doctor to turn the focus on me. I couldn't hear his words as anything but harsh judgment. It seemed he was basically saying, "You seem like you're about to crack, lady." Maybe it wouldn't have been so bad if he hadn't said it in front of Curt.

It took everything I had not to storm out of there. I had just gone through this long journey—mostly alone—and finally discovered that, just as I'd suspected, something was really wrong with Grant. And now the doctor and Curt were making me feel as if I was crazy. I was exasperated. Had we done anything right for our kids?

As we drove home that day, we pulled up to a stoplight right behind a car with a bumper sticker boasting, "My son is an honor roll student at Medfield High!" It was all I could do not to turn into Michael Douglas's character in

Falling Down. I wanted to slam my foot onto the gas pedal, through the floorboard, and into the car in front of me. But I quickly came to my senses. Those people weren't to blame for feeling proud, and what was happening with my kids wasn't their fault. It was mine. Or at least I saw it as mine. Absent someone telling me otherwise, and with a husband I had to kiss good night via AT&T every night, how could I not think this way?

On the ride home, we decided it would be important to tell Gehrig and Gabby about Grant's diagnosis. Because they were the two oldest, we needed them to start changing how they treated Grant immediately. In time we would find the right way to tell Grant, but in the short term, we needed his older siblings to change their behavior.

We were anxious about how they'd take the news. We were wrestling with our own feelings about it, and we had no idea what it would mean to the kids, who, to our knowledge, had even less awareness than we did about Asperger's. But we had to tell them because we needed them to behave differently toward Grant. The way we had all been reacting to him—mostly yelling—had to stop right then and there.

Back in Medfield, we brought Gehrig and Gabby into Curt's office and told them we needed to talk to them about something. Like most kids, their first reaction was "What did I do? Am I in trouble?"

"No, no," Curt assured them. "This is about Grant. We had some tests done on him, and the results show that he is on the spectrum of autism. He has Asperger's."

Both kids had a look of complete shock on their faces. Gabby suddenly started crying.

Interestingly, the kids had more awareness about Asperger's than we did. Who would have guessed that kids would know more than adults about a thing like that? But they'd had kids with autism in their classes since they started school. They'd been exposed to it. They knew firsthand what the differences looked like.

"Actually, it makes sense to me," Gehrig said. "I never could understand why Grant couldn't finish a game with me, or why he'd get bored so quickly when we were doing something together."

Suddenly Gehrig seemed sad. "I feel so bad for all the times I was mean to him," he said. "I realize now that he couldn't help it."

Gabby's reaction was much more emotional. She kept crying.

"I feel horrible for all the times I ever yelled at him to get out of my room," she said, "and for all the times I yelled at him to leave my friends and me alone because he wouldn't stop bothering everyone."

The four of us talked about how Grant's brain is wired differently and about the aspects of Grant's behavior that now made more sense in light of the diagnosis. For instance, we discussed his meltdowns.

"He has those because he can't process what's happening, and he feels as if he's not in control," I explained. "It's going to be important for us to give him his space. And no more calling him a baby or making fun of him. That only makes things worse."

We talked about how the yelling and the name-calling were all in the past. "Now we need to come together as a family and help him," Curt said. "We have to guide him, and also protect him." But most of all, the yelling had to stop, and we needed to start showing more love and patience.

The kids agreed.

Then Gabby said, "I'm afraid that Grant is going to grow up to be lonely and different." I gave her a hug, and cried myself. Though she was only ten, she'd given voice to the same fears I'd felt ever since I'd typed the word *autism* into Google.

Despite our collective anxiety, seeing Gehrig's and Gabby's reactions told me that Curt and I had done the right thing by telling them first. They were both mature enough to use this information to help their brother, at least until the whole family had a better understanding of the kinds of changes this diagnosis would bring.

The lingering question now was how and when to tell Grant. While we wanted desperately for him to understand what he was going through, we also wanted to make sure we handled this with the utmost care, and in order to do that we needed to have a better sense of the facts ourselves. Together Curt and I decided to wait until we could do more research into the right way of sharing the news with Grant. That would give us time to get a better handle on Asperger's in general and make sure that when we finally did tell Grant, we'd do it in a way that would be right for him.

———•———

IT DIDN'T TAKE ME long to look around online and realize that where the diagnosis of straight autism had seemed off, the profile of kids with Asperger's fit Grant perfectly. I felt as if the people writing on those websites had met Grant and described him to a tee.

The syndrome was named for Dr. Hans Asperger, a pediatrician in Vienna, who in 1944 was the first to write about this neurological condition that he had noticed in some children he had observed. What I read over and over again was that kids with Asperger's have different neurological wiring than most people, and that it dramatically affects their ability to understand social cues and their processing of various kinds of sensory stimuli. It isn't an illness but a developmental disorder. And it isn't something you cure—it's something you learn to accommodate and compensate for.

The first and most obvious characteristic is an inability to read social cues. Kids with Asperger's find it hard—painful, even—to look people in the eye, and even when they can, they don't pick up on other people's facial expressions. As a consequence, many of them don't know how to have reciprocal conversations, and lack a normal sense of personal boundaries.

I thought about Grant chasing and poking kids older than he was—kids he didn't know, who didn't want to be bothered, and didn't understand why this kid was poking them—and also about the way he used to like to scare us.

There was also his penchant for talking incessantly at dinner without letting anyone respond to him or break in, and his insistence on telling the same "funny" story over and over. It didn't matter that we kept saying, "We heard it already, Grant. It's not funny anymore."

The other most common feature of Asperger's is sensory issues. Kids with Asperger's don't have normal integrated sensory experiences. Instead, they experience the sensations around any given situation in a disjointed way. That makes some kids need to go further into certain sensations, while others need to withdraw from them. That's part of why Grant can't handle certain textures of food and why he strongly resists foods he's not familiar with.

Scenes from the last seven years of my life kept fading in and out as I revisited them with newfound understanding. Suddenly I understood why Grant liked apples but vehemently hated applesauce. It also explained why he could never handle a lot of noise, and why he had such a hard time at ball games, always covering his ears and rocking until he could put himself to sleep. It was also why we couldn't take him to concerts. We tried many times to go as a family to hear live music, but Grant would freak out every time, screaming, *"I want to go home, now!"* Grant also has big issues with touch. After reading what I did, I began to understand why he needed to touch everything—*everything*—wherever we were, and why he needed to slam his body into me. I have also since learned that he sleeps better at night when he has a special extra-heavy blanket. The pressure helps to calm his nerves.

There's also a tendency among Asperger's kids to wander off and be fearless, regardless of the setting and safety concerns. For a long time I've known that when we go places, I need to have my attention locked in on Grant because if he suddenly sees a dog he wants to pet, he'll just wander that way and get lost from us. (He has a crazy love for all animals, as do most kids with Asperger's. Somehow, animals calm them.) A trick I'd begun practicing before the diagnosis was either to dress him in a really bright color or to put all the kids in the same shirt when we traveled. That way if he disappeared, I would have no question about what he was wearing. Plus, other people would tend to take notice that the kids were dressed alike, which made it easier to get people to help me find him.

Asperger's kids often have an inability to focus consistently, and they become easily distracted. When Grant is playing sports, he will sometimes suddenly become distracted. He'll be standing out in the field with no idea what is going on. On the other hand, kids like Grant can become sharply focused on things they're interested in. He can get lost in his Legos and Chaotic cards for hours on end. This single-mindedness often leads Asperger's kids to excel in fields that interest them—often science and computers (or in Grant's case, dinosaurs). It's insane that Curt missed this for so long, given that I could have replaced Grant's name with Curt's in the sentences above. It's one of the reasons I think he was so good in high-pressure situations. His ability to lock in and focus at those times was incredible.

The inability to stay focused except on certain subjects has another effect: It makes it hard for kids with Asperger's to engage in tasks that have multiple steps. For Grant and many other kids, the first place this difficulty shows up is in a failure to learn how to tie their shoes.

Instructions as simple as "Go upstairs, brush your teeth, and put your PJs on" were for Grant a complicated three-step process. The process had to be broken down: Go upstairs. Brush your teeth. Put your PJs on. Once he got it, he had to repeat it exactly the same way so he wouldn't be anxious about getting it wrong. Go upstairs. Brush his teeth. Put his PJs on. Rinse and repeat, every single night.

Because Asperger's kids have difficulty processing more than one thing at a time, they also don't handle transitions well. They don't know what information and tasks they'll need to process when they're called upon to go different places, or shift to different scenarios, so they prefer to stay put. Just try getting Grant to go anywhere, whether it's soccer practice or the ice cream shop after he's told you he wants ice cream. He hates moving from point A to point B. It was an especially big problem when Curt was still playing and we often traveled to see him, whether at spring training or at an away game. Every car or plane trip with Grant was first met with a protest on his part. Now I know why. I read that experts suggest letting kids with Asperger's know way in advance about any transitions they will need to make, so they can adjust more easily.

One characteristic that makes many outsiders think Asperger's is just an excuse for stubborn behavior, or for parents who are simply indulgent, is that the kids can often only deal with things on their own terms. This is also the characteristic that unfortunately can get people with Asperger's fired from jobs later in life if they don't learn to control it. The perfect example of this occurred when Grant went through his neurological testing. He negotiated every detail of the tests with the woman administering them. He would only read what she asked if he could sit with his feet in the air. I now know he wasn't just giving her a hard time. He was trying to feel safe; he needed to know that he was in control of all the sensory input coming at him, so that nothing would take his senses by surprise.

It was both comforting and upsetting to read these Web sites. On the one hand they offered a clear explanation of why my son acted the way he did. On the other hand it hurt to realize how clueless I'd been about my own child and how I hadn't been doing right by him. I could only read so much, a little at a time.

———————

DESPITE THE INITIAL CONFUSION, guilt, and regret that I felt, it was amazing how one piece of information could change so much. Getting Grant's diagnosis transformed everything—our understanding of him, our reactions to him, and our approach to his care and education. There was a shift in perspective under way from the minute I heard the words *spectrum of autism* and then *Asperger's syndrome*.

The first thing I did was to ignore the neurologist's suggestion not to label Grant in his school file. I understood his rationale, but I knew it didn't make sense for me. In fact, I took the opposite approach: I didn't know how to begin to handle Grant's Asperger's, so I went right to the school, told them all about it, and asked them for help. I felt I had to let them know. How else were they going to be able to help him? Besides, that school administrator I'd talked to in the parking lot before Grant's official diagnosis could clearly see what was going on with him.

My instinct was right. It turned out that the school had services available for kids with Asperger's and autism. It's a public school—all my kids go to public school—and I was pleased to learn that those kinds of services were available there. I've always felt it was important for my kids to be in public schools, to be part of the community.

Grant could go on either an Independent Education Plan (IEP) or a 504 plan. Both programs would take him out of the classroom occasionally for special services and provide accommodations—like an aide to help him focus—inside the classroom. But an IEP is more geared toward learning issues. Grant's issues are more behavioral and don't affect his ability to learn, so he was assigned a 504. That could change as he gets older. We'll see.

The administrator was incredibly helpful, and I knew almost immediately that ignoring the doctor in this case had been the right move. She called a team meeting with Grant's teachers, the principal, and the specialist who worked full-time at the school, to put together a plan that would help Grant get what he needed. I figured the meeting would give me a good chance to learn techniques to help Grant from the professionals themselves as they outlined the regimen that would be best for him. I had the idea before I went that I was composed and put together enough to talk with strangers about Grant's diagnosis, but then I got to the meeting and started falling apart.

In between sniffles, I sat quietly and listened to each of them speak.

Everything they said felt like it was coming at me too quickly. They each had so much to say, and they just rattled it all off. So many different thoughts run through your head at a moment like that. *He's going to be one of those kids people make fun of. His life will be so much more challenging than other kids'. I won't be able to protect him from the other kids.*

I was still worried about even telling Grant that he had Asperger's. We hadn't done that yet, and now there were going to be changes in his schedule at school. But we were only two weeks into the school year, so his routine wasn't firmly set. And the people at the meeting assured me that many kids left the classroom during the day to go to "specials." It's quite different now than it was when I was in school. Back then, everyone knew when a kid was leaving to go get help with speech or reading, and it was a little embarrassing. These days, though, they also refer to "specials" outside the regular classroom as "clubs." They promised me he'd just see it as part of his schedule, but I was still a wreck.

Of course, because of baseball Curt wasn't there with me, and I had to shoulder this all by myself. It didn't take long for everyone at the table to see that this information was more than I could handle. Human nature kicked in, and this band of educators shifted gears into their roles as women and mothers. They reached out to me as moms and tried to make me feel better.

"He will be fine," several of them said, almost in unison. "We'll help him."

Ironically, I have friends whose children have learning issues or are on the autistic spectrum and so have IEPs. Each of my friends offered to go with me. They've been in this game for years, and probably would have provided tremendous support for me at the meeting. But I told them no, I could handle it, thank you, that I was just going for an evaluation. I think deep down I was scared and thought that if they were there, they would push me too much. I needed to experience this at my own pace. In my mind, I hadn't fully accepted what was happening. And I didn't know how to learn. I'd never been the kind of person who goes out and reads everything there is to know about something like this. I wanted something that was simple and straightforward enough that I could deal with it in my current emotional state.

After the meeting, a woman named Kathy handed me the number of another Medfield mom. "Call Christine," she said. "She knows what you're going through. She has a child a year ahead of yours."

I couldn't even properly thank her because I was so afraid I would start crying again. What is it about kindness when you are on the verge of tears that can make you fall apart so easily? As much as I appreciated the gesture, I wasn't ready to reach out and talk to another mother. I was too anxious about the diagnosis to learn too much about it all at once. I could only take information in piecemeal, in stages, and I wasn't ready for the next stage yet.

This was going to take a major adjustment on my part. Life was not going according to plan. I wasn't ready, and honestly I didn't realize how big an adjustment I had to make. The neurologist's advice that I get myself some help kept echoing in my head. There was no way I was going to take his advice. It still felt like an insult. Besides, I was the one who always held things together for everyone else's benefit. If I were to face my grief I would fall apart, and then who would help everyone else keep it together? Seeking help of any kind for myself was out of the question. I kept thinking, *I'm going to continue to appear to be the person people expect me to be. I'm going to be the wife who is smiling in the stands and cheering my husband on, and I'm going to do it without anybody knowing what's going on at home, and in my heart.*

eight
Opening Up

＊

ALL THIS DRAMA WITH OUR FAMILY WAS OCCURRING AT THE
same time as a very different kind of drama—namely, that of the intense and
exciting baseball season—and postseason—of 2007, when Curt played a big
role in taking the Red Sox to another World Series victory.

The whole summer before Grant's diagnosis, as each week of summer
camp and Pop Warner football seemed to reveal something else worrisome
about his behavior, baseball had been my salvation. It provided me with a
much-needed source of fun and distraction—at least as long as Curt and the
team were doing well. And that season, they definitely were. One thing you
have to get used to when you come to the Red Sox is that there is a pretty good
chance your season won't be limited to the typical 162 games. Ownership did
its best to put a winning team on the field, and the Red Sox fans expected
nothing less from their players (a noticeable change since 2004). It was just
the kind of environment my husband thrives on.

And despite all the craziness with our family, it was the kind of environment I thrived on as well. What wouldn't be fun about my summer? Most days

I had the option of either watching my kids play sports or, when they didn't have a game, watching the Red Sox. Sometimes, if the kids didn't have games or activities, we could even fit in a road trip or two. A couple of nights at a hotel watching movies and ordering from room service—oh, and a baseball game thrown in (for everyone but Grant, of course)—sounded pretty good to the kids and me. It was a great chance for us to regroup as a family. I loved disappearing from our life like that. No one could find me, and it almost felt like everyone knew not to call.

Of course, it was not all fun and games on the road when Curt was pitching. On days when he pitched a night game, that meant he slept till noon, got up and ate his same meal of Ellio's pizza, and then took a nap. In a small hotel room, that usually meant I had to take the kids out for a walk so he could rest, although we had to make sure we were back in time for each of the kids to wish Curt good luck, and for me to give him one of my corny poems. That had been our long-standing ritual for many years, whether we were home or away.

That particular summer, when I was so overwhelmed with all this news about my kids, going to the ballpark was my one indulgence. Being in public provided an opportunity for me to be "on." I became a different person, a person for whom everything was always just fine. When Curt had pitched for other teams, a few of the fans had known who the wives were and occasionally said hello. But Red Sox Nation was different. From the minute we were traded, they knew a lot about me. And they all felt as if they really *knew* me. I couldn't maneuver my way through the stadium without making lots of small talk with fans. And that summer the fans thankfully kept me busy. I've always loved my conversations with the fans, but that summer, for the first time, I felt like I really needed them. Who would have wanted to hear my problems when the Red Sox were in first place? In Red Sox world, that's like being sad on Christmas.

So that's what I did that summer when everything was falling apart. I went to the ballpark and smiled my way through the pain I was feeling before and after Grant's diagnosis in August. I didn't have to think about what was going on off the field or what would happen when the lights on the field went dark. If I could go to the ballpark and pretend everything was okay, then I wouldn't have to feel or think about what was really going on. I wouldn't have to feel so guilty about not noticing Grant's differences sooner or not getting him diagnosed earlier.

Not even some of my closest friends knew the full extent of what I was going through, and in public I did everything I could to keep it all to myself. My parents taught me at an early age that you never knew what was going on in someone else's home and so you should never assume anything. Growing up in a row house, if your neighbors were arguing, chances were you heard it. No one ever mentioned those arguments in public, though. People kept those things to themselves. That summer I learned what my parents meant—you never know what's really going on in someone else's home, and in their inner life.

<hr/>

WE DECIDED TO TAKE the kids out of school for that World Series. We knew that Curt's career was coming to an end, and even if he came back for 2008, there was no guarantee that we would make it back to the World Series again. We wanted the kids to be a part of this experience and see as much as they could.

Of course, Grant made things more complicated. I tried to take him to see game three. Curt was not pitching, and the Sox were up two games to zero. But it didn't work. He was restless and noisy, and to make matters worse, Garrison had started following his lead, so my dad took Grant home for me. To Grant, this game wasn't any different. That it was something really special didn't compute for him. As far as he was concerned, it might as well have been a Little League game.

After we won game three, my parents and I came up with a plan for game four: They would bring Grant and Garrison in during the seventh inning. Though I'd only just begun to learn about Asperger's, I knew how important it is to explain an environment and expectations before the child arrives in a particular situation. That improves your chances of having some control—although there are no guarantees.

After the seventh inning stretch, I took Grant up in the stands and explained to him, with each and every play, what he could expect. My parents and I told him what a big deal the World Series was and how many people were watching the game around the world. As the final innings progressed, I talked him through play by play so that he could try to get a sense of what was coming next. I knew that when the last out was made, it would be very loud, and there was a good chance Grant wouldn't be able to handle the noise. I let him know that it would become very loud because people would be cheering, and there might also be fireworks.

When the last out was made, I literally held my breath for a second and silently prayed, *Please don't freak out,* before I looked at Grant. When I finally looked over at him, I was shocked to see him jumping up and down. He started screaming himself, and then he began hugging everyone. He was just excited. He was even more excited than the rest of us.

For a minute I felt as if I were frozen in time. After the last few months, just being able to sit back and watch Grant's euphoria made me almost as happy as the fact that we'd just won the World Series. Nothing will ever compare to witnessing Grant's excitement and joy, and the feeling of relief that came over me. In that moment it didn't matter that Grant couldn't name anyone on the team, or that he hadn't been able to sit through games before. Right then he was sharing his pure joy with us, and it warmed my heart as nothing else could. The fact that he was able to share this moment with all of us, that he was able to be just as excited as the millions of other Red Sox fans who were losing their minds, told me that we were going to get through this.

What I will remember the most about that night was seeing all the players' kids on the field, hugging their dads, taking pictures with all our friends and teammates. It was a real celebration for everyone. Everyone but Grant.

He had discovered himself on Fan-O-Vision in center field and was running back and forth, watching himself on the screen. He couldn't connect to what was happening on the field with all of us. But that was okay. I remember thinking, *He's happy. He's different, but he's okay.*

———•———

THE DOWNSIDE TO ALL the baseball excitement that year was that it meant Curt was unavailable for serious parenting almost all the way into November, which made it all the more difficult to implement the necessary changes that Grant's Asperger's diagnosis required of both of us as parents. The World Series win was followed by a parade, and before I knew it, Thanksgiving, Christmas, and New Year's were right around the corner. We had to read and learn and get involved in special programs, but we also had to find the time to do it together as parents.

It was an adjustment for the rest of the family as well. Even though we still hadn't told Grant, there were changes we all had to get used to. The most pronounced change was that the yelling stopped. I understood very clearly that when we were trying to get Grant to do something, no matter how frustrating it got, I couldn't lose my patience and raise my voice. Neither could Curt. It took awhile, but that fall I worked hard to keep my voice in check. (I have now become so patient, there are times I'm sure people want to check my pulse and make sure I'm alive—especially bystanders who see Grant giving me a hard time.)

A couple of days after the New Year, with no more distractions to keep me from digging in, I started learning more about Asperger's. My research began online, and as I started looking for resources around us, up popped an e-mail address for a contact in our area. Lo and behold, it was the address of Christine, the mom the administrator had told me to call back in September. Without thinking, I sent Christine an e-mail. To me, an e-mail seemed safer and less complicated than a phone call. On the phone it would be awkward and difficult if I couldn't handle what she had to say, or if I felt I had to keep the conversation going. I hate dead air, so I talk constantly when I meet a new person. Just my luck, though—that e-mail address no longer worked. I found a certain relief in that, and took it as a sign that I must not really be ready to talk to someone outside my immediate circle.

But in my mind, I couldn't let go of it. I had a whole cold, gray January to ruminate on it. I had nothing but time during that month of the year. Curt wouldn't be leaving for spring training until February. It was one of those rare occasions when we were a two-parent home with no holidays. With the extra breathing room, I couldn't stop thinking about how I should call that woman Christine. *Make the phone call,* I kept telling myself. *You are ready.* Finally, one afternoon I looked up her phone number and gave her a call.

Talking to her, I immediately felt more at ease. I was no longer alone. We shared stories about our sons. What I remember most was that she said her son had a couple of good friends that he played with. I was so afraid of Grant not having friends. Ever since that first failed playdate back when he was in preschool, I had been avoiding playdates for Grant, and I was excited to learn that it could work. Here was a part of his life that might possibly be normal and typical. Until that moment, every piece of information that I'd heard or read had been about the ways he'd always be different.

We talked for a good hour. Christine told me about her connection with the Asperger's Association of New England, and filled me in on how many kids in our town alone were on the spectrum of autism. I was quite shocked. Not only was I not alone on this ship, but I had *lots* of company—nearby, no less. The one thing I had been avoiding for months was what I needed most: to connect with other people facing the same thing. I needed to hear someone say that Grant would ultimately be okay, and I needed that to come not from a doctor or a teacher but from a parent who knew from her own experience. I needed to hear someone tell me, "Yes, life will be challenging at times, but he will be okay."

Back during my first meeting about Grant with Dr. Rosenberger, he told me that Grant would most likely grow up and get married and have kids. He would probably marry someone who shared his interests. For months I'd been struggling to see this actually happening, but after talking to Christine, all that changed.

That phone call was followed shortly thereafter by a call I made to the Asperger's Association of New England, where a woman named Brenda Dater answered. I asked her several questions, and I could feel myself starting to loosen up. Never once did Brenda mention that she knew who I was or to whom I was married. She never acknowledged she knew until I talked about it first. She knew how I was feeling and talked to me like a friend.

Brenda had *two* children with Asperger's. I was having such a hard time with one, I couldn't imagine how she handled two. Yet she was happy and proud. Her optimism was infectious and I knew immediately that I needed to find some of her upbeat spirit. Brenda offered to come over and show me some techniques that helped her family. A week later she arrived and we sat talking for two hours. I have to say that what she did in a day, every day, seemed like an awful lot of work. She talked about how kids with Asperger's take comfort in having schedules, and how she makes sure she sets and sticks to a clear-cut agenda for her kids. I imagined her house filled with schedules and charts.

One of the most valuable lessons I took away from that day with Brenda was what she called her "one to five." It was a scale of emotional responses, and the idea was to help the child correlate his or her reactions to the appropriate number. For example, not liking what you're told to do—like having to turn off your computer game and brush your teeth when you'd rather not—warranted a level-one reaction: maybe a little resistance and whining. Nothing short of a fire or other emergency warranted a level-five reaction, which might include screaming, crying inconsolably, and what I would call a total meltdown. It's natural for kids with Asperger's to go straight to level five over the smallest things, and Grant was no exception.

The one-to-five scale was a concrete way for me to give Grant a sense of what was appropriate behavior. Did it work the first time? No. But now I only have to say, "Is not being able to get the toy you want right now cause for level-five behavior or level-one?"

Suddenly I felt as if I'd been hired for a new job. We had just finished orientation for my new motherhood position, and I had a lot of retraining to go through. It wasn't easy to remember all of it, but I was trying. From the moment I started talking to Christine and Brenda, I felt as if I was taking my life back. No one else was going to help Grant. I had to.

———·———

AFTER BRENDA DATER CAME to my house, she told me I should try to attend a support group meeting. It seemed like a good idea. But I wasn't going to go alone. I'd learned my lesson after attending that meeting at the school, where I totally broke down.

Since Curt was at spring training, and my mother was eager to learn all she could about Grant and his issues, she agreed to go with me. We showed up at the meeting with about four couples. On the table were six or seven really thick books about Asperger's. Each of the people in attendance was giving a review of a book. I just sat quietly and listened as they all spoke eloquently. I felt like I was sitting in on a graduate-level course on the subject. My mom and I later laughed in the car. "Can you imagine what dumb asses we probably looked like to them?" I said. "I looked at those books and thought, 'Let me know when the comic book version comes out.'"

But when my mother and I weren't laughing at ourselves, we compared notes on the parts that were really informative. In truth the meeting wasn't at all stuffy. There was a lot of humor as people shared funny stories about the ways Asperger's had made their kids do strange things. There were poignant moments, too, when people shared their frustrations and struggles. It was a reality check for me to discover that there were others with bigger struggles than I had. It made me feel grateful that my child liked school, his teachers liked him, and his school administrators were good to me.

The group discussed various aspects of Asperger's. They talked about how some people think it's the result of early childhood vaccinations, although people in the group generally believed that to be a myth. I figure, my other kids got the same vaccinations, and they don't have Asperger's. Also, the group touched on the diet changes that some in the world of alternative medicine recommend—namely, a gluten-free, caseine-free diet—as a way of managing or even "curing" Asperger's. The consensus of the group was that even if there are benefits, they are not significant enough to warrant the difficulty of trying to keep your kid away from most normal foods. Not to mention the stigma of a special diet added to the stigma of being different.

One topic came up that caught me way off guard, though. Someone in the group mentioned that Asperger's kids have a high incidence of teen suicide. At the moment I heard it, I thought about how lucky I was that Grant was only in the third grade, and so I didn't have to worry now about him being ostracized as a teen and feeling so bad he'd want to kill himself. Other than that thought, I didn't react in the meeting.

I didn't think much more about the meeting until the next day. I was on the Asperger's Association Web site looking up something we'd talked about. Something there led me to a link about Asperger's kids and teen suicide, and I lost it. Once again I was crying. I was so sad and scared. I called Curt and told him about it.

"Curt, how will I ever protect Grant from the world?" I asked, sobbing. "Who has the right to ever make anyone feel that low about himself?"

Curt tried to console me, long-distance, but I couldn't get that awful topic out of my head. It brought up the memory of my maternal grandfather, who had killed himself when I was sixteen. I'm haunted by that day, when my father and I came home from the beach to find a cop car parked in front of the house. My father was driving, and I remember vividly how we both jumped out of the car and sprinted for the door, where we found my mother inside the house, lying on the floor screaming near where my grandfather, a recovering alcoholic, had shot himself. A policeman was trying to get my mother to drink water. They sent me upstairs, and as I walked slowly up to my room, my mother's cries pierced my ears, lingering in the air for what seemed like days.

I couldn't seem to think straight, when the phone rang. It was Brenda. "So what did you think of the meeting?" she asked.

"Well," I said, "I'm really struggling. That bit about teen suicide really scared me."

Brenda tried to calm me down. "It doesn't have to be like that, Shonda," she told me. "We are making changes in this world. We're making progress, and hopefully there will be more awareness and acceptance by the time Grant is in his teens." She assured me I had done a good thing by coming to the meeting. "You're doing a good job for Grant, preparing him for the world."

———·———

OVER THE NEXT MONTH, I talked to several more people about Asperger's—some who had kids on the spectrum and some who didn't. Many kept recommending a special camp called YouthCare, which was affiliated with Massachusetts General Hospital. When one person mentioned to me that I should check out YouthCare I thought, *Okay, sure*, and added it to my long list of things to look into. But when a second and a third person also recommended YouthCare, I realized I had to take this recommendation seriously.

The first thing I learned about it was how close it was to our house—only about fifteen minutes away. Considering all the trouble Grant had gotten into at regular day camp, I liked the idea of him being close enough for me to intervene if things didn't go well. I thought, *Well, of all the camps in Boston, at least this one is close by.*

But there was so much more to it. When I did a little research into it, and then met with people there, I discovered that YouthCare was truly one of a kind. The camp has been around for about twenty years, working with kids with Asperger's and autism since way before the conditions were diagnosed so commonly. The people there are dedicated to those kids and are incredibly knowledgeable about their issues. Scott McLeod, the executive director, has been involved with YouthCare for nineteen years and has run the organization for six. That's commitment. These people clearly believe that what they're doing is important.

The more I learned, the more I wanted Grant to benefit from this incredible system. I quickly applied for enrollment in the summer camp, and after a short time, they called and asked for an interview. I felt as if I had hit the jackpot. A summer camp experience for kids with Asperger's, where they'd teach them skills for coping in life, and it was only fifteen minutes away? It sounded like a dream come true

I took Grant to the interview, and for the first time in my life, I was afraid he would be too well behaved and that because they wouldn't recognize his issues they wouldn't take him. Grant is very high-functioning, and he can be very charming, especially with adults. Besides, this seemed too good to be true. Something just had to go wrong.

We arrived at the interview and began to talk to the administrator. Grant did what he does all the time: He touched every single thing in that office. He didn't look at the administrator and could barely respond to her questions. He was in his own world. Walking into this room filled with all this new stuff just drew his attention away from what was going on.

I had no idea what the administrator was thinking. I couldn't help but anxiously wonder, *Would we get in or not?* After we'd been in her office a while, she clued me in.

"I have one spot open," she said. "There's a group that has five boys with different variations of social issues. Grant would be a year younger than the others, but I still think he'd be a perfect fit."

I was so excited, and proud, too. I felt as if Grant had just been accepted to Harvard.

I later told her, "You know, I had been afraid Grant would be too charming and well-behaved at the meeting, camouflaging his issues. I was afraid he wouldn't get in."

"Oh, no," she said. "I could tell within two minutes of seeing him that Grant had Asperger's."

I was floored. What took me almost seven years to figure out took her just two minutes. At once I felt grateful, hopeful—and like an incompetent parent. All over again.

With the acceptance at the camp came a new realization: It was time for Curt and me to tell Grant about his Asperger's. It had been building for months now as I piled on more and more information, and both Curt and I finally felt ready to tackle the task of talking to him. We'd been talking to several other families about how they'd handled it and we felt confident that now was the time. All of us in the family (with the exception of Garrison, who also didn't know) had been changing their attitudes toward Grant for the last few months, and he needed to understand why. Also, we were going to start giving him certain kinds of advice to help him, and it only made sense for us to tell him why. Not to mention that he would be going to a special camp, and would probably ask why none of his siblings were going.

We also decided that this was something that could not be done one-on-one with Grant. We didn't want it to seem as though we were hiding this or that it was private. Of course, Gehrig and Gabby knew, but we wanted Grant to see from the beginning that we were all in this together to help him. Grant's Asperger's was something we needed to deal with as a family, and one night at dinner with the whole family we broke the news.

"Grant, your mind works a little differently from ours," Curt explained. "It's because your brain is wired differently. It's not bad—it's just different."

"You're very smart," I added. "You're very funny and loving, too. But sometimes you do stuff that people just don't understand, and that has to do with your different brain wiring."

As an example, we mentioned the way he often talked over everyone. "You know how we're always stopping you from talking, and trying to get you to give others a chance?" I asked.

"Yeah," he said, nodding his head.

"Well, that's the sort of thing that most people know how to do. It just comes to them naturally. For you, it's different."

Surprisingly, Grant was not fazed at all. Garrison either. I was pleased.

"As a family, we've decided to all help you when you're doing something that other people might not understand," Curt told him. He seemed fine with that. We decided to try and come up with a family code word. Whenever we said that word, Grant would know to stop whatever it was he was doing.

This is where the conversation took a sharp turn away from the mature, intellectual discussion I'd been hoping for.

"Hey, how about we say 'Turd knocker,' so you'll know to stop!" Gehrig suggested.

"Or what if we say, 'You're a booger,'" Gabby said, laughing. This code word thing was not going to happen.

I had prepared myself for the possibility that Grant would be upset by this topic, but surprisingly, he was excited. He seemed to feel good about the whole family taking such an interest in him. He loved the attention and didn't give a second thought to having been told he was different. It seemed he really didn't care.

As I cleared the table that night, I kept thinking, *That was just too easy.* It had been a long time since something felt too easy when it came to Grant.

nine
One Happy Camper

WHILE I FELT I WAS MAKING A LOT OF PROGRESS IN UNDER-standing Asperger's and opening myself up to the ideas and techniques that I needed to relearn as a parent, the bad news was that once again I was doing it all without Curt. In February 2008 he went to spring training, so he wasn't around to learn alongside me or to help with Grant. He also wasn't there to see what was happening with Gehrig at dinnertime.

Dinnertime in my house had never been terribly easy. Because of all our traveling as a baseball family, my kids got very used to eating at restaurants on the run and ordering whatever they wanted from room service in hotels. The menu rarely strayed far from grilled cheese, peanut butter and jelly, and of course, ballpark hot dogs. The concept of everyone eating the same food, at our own dinner table, was introduced late in the game—probably not until we moved to Massachusetts. My kids have very limited palates, which, I'm sorry to say, they get from their father. Vegetables are a very hard sell all around.

We always had an especially hard time getting Grant to eat what was being served. Before his diagnosis, we had no idea why, but he would arbitrarily refuse to eat certain foods. After we found out about Asperger's, we came to understand that some foods he won't eat because of his sensory issues, which cause him to hate certain textures. But there have always been other foods he'd reject that we knew he loved—mashed potatoes, for instance. He'd become completely obsessed with a food like that for a while and want to eat it at every meal, every day. Then all at once he'd snap out of the obsession and refuse to eat it. Sometimes he'd request a food for dinner—pork chops, maybe. And then when it was being served that very night, he'd recoil from it. Of course, he'd probably wait until you put it on the table to change his mind.

Even when he wasn't digging his heels in and refusing to eat, Grant was usually too busy talking to take in enough nourishment. He talked and talked and talked over everybody. One of the by-products of his inability to read social cues is that he didn't understand how to have a normal conversation. In the same way he didn't know to give other kids turns sliding down the slide at a pool, he didn't know to let other people speak.

In the past, our misguided way of dealing with Grant's refusal to eat was to yell at him.

"*Grant, eat that!*" I would shout.

"*No!*" he'd shout back.

"*Eat that now or you're not leaving the table!*" Curt would shout. For some reason, I'd get angry at Curt for shouting, even though I was doing the same exact thing. Maybe it was because he was so much louder than I was. So we'd scream and make Grant eat. He'd cry and cry. And then he'd throw it up. Right there, at the table.

Once we understood that there was a reason Grant was being so strange about food, the first thing we did was stop yelling at him, but it would be a while before we learned how to get him to eat enough and stop talking over everyone. Still, at least the yelling stopped.

But just as the yelling at dinner was stopping, a new problem was starting;

namely, Gehrig was now refusing to eat. Only it wasn't as obvious as that.

I'd first noticed that there was something strange going on with Gehrig and food during the spring of 2007, around the time he was diagnosed with ADHD. Seemingly out of the blue, I'd realized that both Grant and Gabby both ate more then Gehrig did. I mentioned it once in a while.

"Gehrig, how can you not finish that hamburger?" I'd ask him as he pushed aside the food I'd gotten him at the McDonald's drive-through. "Garrison is five, and even he can eat a McDonald's cheeseburger. Why can't you?"

When we were at sporting events, I would listen to stories parents told about their boys—Gehrig's age—starting to eat everything in the house. I rationalized to myself that Gehrig had been a May baby. He was a little bit younger than some of the kids, so maybe it was okay that he was a later bloomer. But I didn't completely buy my own argument. I started to talk to my mom, my girlfriends, and Curt about it. No one else seemed alarmed, but my gut just didn't feel right. Once again I felt people second-guessing my instincts as a mother, and I didn't like that. So I made an appointment with the doctor at the beginning of that summer.

"I don't think Gehrig eats enough for his age," I said to the doctor.

"Well," she said, after examining him carefully, "if he doesn't gain a pound or grow an inch by the end of the summer, we'll run some tests. But don't worry about it."

That worked for me. I could give it a couple of months. But then, when I got home, my mind went right to the bad place. I had met too many families with sick kids in all my years of baseball and had filled out too much paperwork around my melanoma diagnosis to forget that weight loss and loss of appetite are symptoms of some forms of cancer. I didn't want to put my mind there, but those thoughts couldn't help but linger.

That was also the summer Gehrig's younger sister grew five inches. I swear, in the past she would grow and two days later he would wake up and be the same height. It bothered Gehrig terribly that Gabby was now taller than he was. No matter how many times I tried to explain that sometimes girls grow earlier than boys, it didn't ease Gehrig's pain.

That summer, when Gehrig played Pop Warner football, he seemed to have a better appetite. That made me feel a little better. At the end of the summer I took him to the doctor again. He'd grown half an inch and gained one pound.

"He didn't lose weight," the doctor pointed out. "He may not have grown or gained a lot, but he is moving in the right direction."

She didn't feel that there was a problem. I was able to exhale for the first time in a while. Sitting all summer with this gnawing suspicion that something was seriously wrong had worn on me. When the 2007 school year started and Gehrig resumed throwing away his Adderall pills, I called the doctor to ask whether it was possible that it could really leave a bad taste in his mouth.

"Absolutely not," she said.

I couldn't understand why Gehrig was trying to control this so much. He and I got into fights over it.

"You need to take the medication, Gehrig," I argued.

"Why do I have to?!" he'd shout. *"I don't want to!"*

"Well, at least stop throwing them away in places where your little brothers and the dogs can get them," I said, and gave up on trying to get him to take his medicine.

Things had continued on like that until around February 2008. Then one night I was eating at a restaurant with Gehrig, his friend Joey, and Joey's mother, and I watched silently as Gehrig pushed his food all over the plate without ever taking a bite. Meanwhile, Joey seemed to inhale his food in what seemed like a series of large gulps.

"Why aren't you eating?" I finally asked.

"I don't like this food," he answered. It was a comment I had been hearing way too often.

I was upset. I'd just watched his friend eat everything on his plate and then start picking at ours. I went home that night and called Curt at spring training.

"Curt, something is just not right with Gehrig and his eating," I said.

"Don't worry about it, Shonda," Curt said dismissively. "He'll eat when he's hungry."

I was right back to where I'd been ten months before, when I wanted to take Gehrig in for ADHD testing, and four months before, when I'd noticed differences in Grant. Once again Curt was doubting my instincts, and it made me so mad I wanted to scream.

I searched my mind for reasons Gehrig might have stopped eating. Was he upset that Curt had left again for spring training? Was it because Grant was now getting more attention and being treated more leniently because of his Asperger's? Was it because of a girl? I just wanted to make sure he knew he could talk to me about anything. Over the next two months, I would ride Gehrig all the time about eating. I didn't care *what* he ate, as long as he did. He could eat cereal for breakfast, lunch, and dinner if he wanted for all I cared.

Dinner became more of a nightmare than ever before. Between Grant not wanting to eat certain foods and Gehrig not eating anything, I was defeated before I got to the table. Besides, how could I enforce dinner rules for Gabby and Garrison if I couldn't make the others eat?

———

CURT RETURNED HOME FROM spring training, and before I knew it the 2008 season had begun. I think the people of New England love opening day so much because they know it means that spring is here and the cold, snowy winter is coming to an end. But for me, as the baseball season started, I felt like I was a bomb waiting to go off. All I needed was the spark.

I knew something was wrong, and my feeling got stronger and stronger.

I never thought for one second, *He's a boy and this doesn't happen with boys*. I knew something was going on. I kept talking to people about it—my friends, my parents, Curt, doctors. The only person who seemed to understand what I was saying was my mom. Meanwhile, Curt continued to think that nothing was wrong, which just infuriated me more.

On top of all the kids' issues, Curt was feuding with the Red Sox over an injury he'd sustained during the 2007 season. As he had in past off-seasons, Curt ramped up his throwing and exercising, starting in just before the new year began. One day in early 2008, he came home from one of his workouts and told me that his shoulder hurt. Of course, as soon as the Red Sox found out, they were furious.

Curt went for X-rays and an MRI on the shoulder. The Red Sox didn't believe there was any kind of a tear, in contrast to the opinion of Dr. Craig Morgan, the surgeon who had performed career-saving surgeries on Curt's shoulder in 1995 and 1999. That's when the disagreement with management started. Curt knew there was something seriously wrong with his shoulder and thought he needed surgery. He brought the films to a few different doctors for other opinions, but none of them could see anything on them either. As the 2008 season inched closer, the Red Sox decided that Curt would rehab the arm until midseason and then see what the doctor's prognosis was. They were hoping physical therapy would do the trick. Curt knew it wouldn't.

"I know my arm," he argued, "and I'm telling you that if you let me have surgery now, I can pitch toward the end of the season, and the season won't be lost."

But the Red Sox physicians didn't agree. Curt had to be at the ballpark every day to maintain their rehab schedule.

In late April the Red Sox were playing the Orioles in Baltimore and I flew down for the night. I was giving a speech in Baltimore about sun safety, and it was a great chance for Curt and me to spend a night together alone. Life as a couple had been getting away from us. We were living two completely separate lives under the same roof—when Curt was home. When he was away, we didn't even have the roof in common.

We needed some time alone. Plus, I hadn't been to as many games lately. For the first ten years of our marriage, I went to just about every home game, and not just the ones he pitched in. I was heavily vested in the teams and being a baseball wife. I always believed the wives were their own team, and the importance of being at games my husband didn't pitch in was something he imparted to me from the outset, and something I was proud to do. But with our increasingly complicated home life, I hadn't been going nearly as much this season.

At the same time, Curt's work required so much that we got very little of him. He had to leave every other week. When he was home, he was out cold when the kids left for school because he was still recovering from getting home late after a game. Then he had to leave for the ballpark at one in the afternoon, before the kids got home from school.

It got to the point where living forty-five minutes from Fenway became a blessing. That was our alone-together time each day. I got forty-five minutes to catch him up on four children. That took about forty minutes, and left about five for a catch-up on us. But we had gotten to a place where each of us felt unappreciated by the other for all we did, and it was not fun. Given our competitive natures, it was easy for our conversations to quickly descend into arguments. Someone was on the offense, someone was on the defense, and neither of us gave any ground. The conversations couldn't go anywhere. I think this happens to a lot of couples who are married for a long time, who have stopped really talking.

My side of our phone conversations became ten-minute updates on the house, the kids, and me. At the end of each report, I dared him to question me for my choices and actions. If he did, he was insulting my way of handling motherhood.

Sometimes I'd only call him late at night, or not at all if I was busy. I'd give him the rundown on what was happening with the kids, who wasn't behaving, and how tired and frustrated I was. The problem was, I was talking to someone who was at his wits' end as well. He was frustrated that the team had forced him down a path he knew would get in the way of his ever pitching again. He wanted our calls at night to provide him with a chance to unwind and smile. Instead, he was getting a litany of complaints.

"Why are you calling me with all this bad stuff that I can't do anything about from here?" he asked one night.

"Because I need you to help me with this," I said. "I need your help instilling some discipline around here."

"I hear you," he said, "but I'm not coming home after a ten-day road trip, having only talked to the kids five times, and punishing them. That's what you need to do."

That set me off. Curt wanted to hear that everything was fine. But there I was dealing with Grant's Asperger's, everyone's ADHD, and Gehrig's eating issues all by myself. It left me feeling as if I would always have to face our kids' major issues alone.

Needless to say, our mini-honeymoon in Baltimore was not long enough. In what felt like an instant, we were heading back to reality. As we were getting on the plane to come home, Marlyn, my second set of hands with the kids, called us and said that Gehrig had asked for hamburgers for dinner—and then flushed his down the toilet. The toilet clogged.

That was the spark that set off the time bomb I'd become. "That's *it*!" I said to Curt. "Something is *wrong*! I know it."

I had her put Gehrig on the phone, and I yelled at him. *"I want answers!"* I screamed. *"Why would you throw your dinner away like that?!"* He couldn't give me answers. He didn't seem to know what to say.

After I hung up with Gehrig, as I was getting on the plane, I called the doctor to make an appointment.

At her office, I filled her in on what had happened since I last spoke to her. "I know something is wrong," I told her. "At this point, I don't want to fight with Curt about this."

She looked me in the eye. "It's time for you to be the mother, Shonda!" she said. "Just take control of the situation."

Wow. It sounded so simple, but it hit me like a thunderclap. I needed that smack on the head. It was humiliating that she had to say it to me, but inspiring as well. Apparently I was doubting my instincts as much as everyone else was. Not anymore. I scheduled another appointment for the following day, and made sure that Curt could go. I knew the only way he would understand was if someone other than me said the words.

The appointment was on a Friday afternoon. I reminded Curt by e-mail and by phone. Two hours before the meeting he called to tell me he couldn't make it.

"Fine," I said. "But don't you dare question me or second-guess anything I tell you after the meeting."

Fuming, I picked Gehrig up from school and took him to the doctor's office. Curt was there in the waiting room. We walked in not really speaking to one another. The doctor took Gehrig into the examining room and weighed him. He was seventy-eight pounds and thirteen years old. He had lost two pounds since the summer. My fear was confirmed.

The doctor referred us to an eating disorders specialist. When we arrived at his office, the specialist sat us down. "If Gehrig loses one more pound, we'll have to admit him to the hospital," he said. "He'll have to be hooked up to a feeding tube through his nose."

That thought alone was enough to get Gehrig to eat a little bit. That and the knowledge that he was actually stunting his growth. He wanted to be taller! But he clearly needed more than just that nudge. He needed serious help. He was placed in an intense outpatient program for kids with eating disorders. He would spend three hours a night there, three days a week.

And so would Curt and I. Another subject I didn't want to become educated on. The saving grace in all of this was that Curt finally got his much-needed shoulder surgery. In June, after a few months of Curt telling the Red Sox over and over that his shoulder wasn't getting better, they let him have surgery. When they opened him up, they found that his bicep was actually torn, as he'd been claiming since January. Curt's baseball season was officially over. We would face this one together.

—•—

AS HARD AS THINGS were with Gehrig, the summer had been one of education for me. I was still learning about Asperger's and trying to implement whatever I could to help Grant—and me—enjoy life on a day-to-day basis. Something as simple as a wall calendar would light him up. He needed structure. He really loved school, and I think the schedule and structure of it were what appealed to him. He loved it so much that he attended "early school," a recess session before classes, for the entire year! In a house full of kids who despised school, I had Grant waking himself up early in order to get to early school every day. That meant he would arrive at 7:30 A.M., even though school didn't officially start until 9.

I was incredibly excited about Grant starting his camp, and I shared my excitement about YouthCare with him. I had been told that Asperger's kids do much better in situations where they know what to expect, so I had many conversations with Grant about what he'd find at YouthCare—the swimming, canoeing, tree climbing, hiking, and more. He was excited, too.

We went to orientation several days before the camp started. There we were greeted by a lot of people. Each group would have six kids and two camp leaders. My first thought was, *God bless these people.* I always felt exhausted after one day with Grant; I couldn't even fathom five days a week for eight weeks straight with a whole camp full of Grants. The camp personnel explained how their day would go, how drop-off and pickup would take place, and handed us some papers and lists of things the kids would need for the next eight weeks. Grant was looking forward to getting his camp gear together. He didn't think twice about the fact that he wasn't going to the same camp as his siblings.

The first day came, and Grant was up early. We arrived and waited near the front in the line of cars. Grant's camp counselor came out and greeted him.

"Hey, Grant," he said after I rolled down the window. "You ready for camp?"

"Yes!" Grant exclaimed, and then bounded out of the car. He didn't even kiss me good-bye. I listened as each counselor he passed chirped, "Good morning, Grant!" They greeted all the kids this way. They already knew all the kids by name.

I waited until he was well on his way, and then drove out of the camp-ground. Not even a mile past the exit, I had to pull over. Without warning tears came streaming down my face, only they were tears of joy. I felt as if, for the first time, I'd finally made a good decision for Grant. He was happy and he was safe, and they wanted him. I let out a sigh of relief that was unlike any I'd known—either before or since. In that moment, I knew that I'd done the right thing as his mother.

As I got the hang of Grant's day-to-day routine, I soon learned that what happened at camp didn't just stay there. The people involved were interested in utilizing each kid's experiences to aid parents in helping their kids at home. For example, right from the start of the summer, I received daily notes, sent home with Grant, about what he was working on there. The notes were designed to give the kids goals and to let their parents see their progress. For the most part the notes were encouraging and upbeat. The kids were trying, and for that, they were always praised. I later learned that the staff deliberately use "strength-based" language, with a ratio of at least eight compliments per criticism, to help build a child's confidence. Sometimes the note would say something like "Grant had trouble with transitions today," but it wasn't an admonishment, just something to make him, and us, aware of where he needed more work. These daily notes were crucial for me because they often contained little tips that could immediately be introduced into our home in a way that would elicit positive responses from Grant.

If your behavior was good and you really tried to meet your goals, twice during the summer you were invited for an overnight at the campsite. A couple of times during the summer the parents were invited to a conference. Here the counselors would share the strategies that worked and talk about the ones that didn't work so well. One thing is for sure: I never left the meetings feeling that Grant wasn't trying really hard.

I was amazed by how young the counselors were—kids in their early twenties. They were giving up the summer between semesters at college or graduate school to work with kids like Grant. Sure, they got paid, but many of them hoped to go into careers helping people with Asperger's and autism. Besides being really good at what they did, none of them ever seemed to be down. They loved what they were doing and it showed.

Grant didn't often share a lot about camp. It took mental and physical effort on his part all day, and by the time he got home, he needed to decompress. I'd often leave him alone and let him relax for a while after camp. Usually once he'd relaxed awhile—playing with his Legos or reading about dinosaurs in his room—he was ready for whatever was next in his day, and so revisiting camp didn't happen much.

When he did talk about camp, the subject he touched on the most was swimming. He seemed to be always concerned about each person in his group doing the best they could in the water. Swimming is an area where Grant shines. He's a natural at it and it's a sensory experience he loves. It seemed good for him that he got to be an example and a cheerleader for those who struggled at it.

Each day of camp would begin with a campwide sharing session that would then lead to a group sharing session. Each child would have time to share. Now that might sound simple enough, but in Grant's group, there were six kids, and they all had issues with communication and with letting others be heard. It was a challenge for them to listen respectfully to each other without interrupting and to make eye contact when other people were speaking. They worked on this seemingly simple task all summer long.

The campwide morning meetings featured lessons of the week. Those lessons would be broken down into smaller lessons for each group. First they'd discuss a lesson, then they'd do exercises, and the theme of the lesson would be carried throughout their day.

Learning to respect individual space is one example of a lesson. Kids with Asperger's don't have the same sense of boundaries around individual space that most people have. In the lesson, counselors would explain that, using the term *personal bubble*, and giving the kids visuals to help them understand. They were taught that different people have different-sized bubbles, and that they can change with your mood. They learned that personal bubbles can hold feelings. If you're happy, your bubble might be smaller, which would allow friends and family to come closer to you. If you're angry or upset, your bubble might be larger, which would mean that people needed to stay farther away. After that, they might play a game of tag. A counselor might explain to them that when you're running, your individual bubble is large, but when someone comes closer, that bubble gets smaller. This was helpful for both the kids who tended to come too close to other people and the ones who didn't like to be touched.

In drama class, they would put on plays with themes relating to social interaction. Each kid had a character that related to the issues he or she specifically needed to work on. All summer they worked on their plays, learning their lines, practicing being on stage, and role-playing using props. In arts and crafts, they would make the props and sets for their plays. In order to put the plays on for the parents at the end of the summer, they needed to learn how to work as a team, letting each person say his or her lines without being interrupted. It required them to stay focused in a way that didn't come naturally to them.

There was environmental education, which included doing archery and taking nature hikes. Each child was given a task on each hike; for instance, Grant's job one time was to identify trees. They were also taught how to interact in conversations during their hikes and their walks from one activity to the next. This posed some difficulty for Grant because the camp setting did not shake him from his tendency to wander. Sometimes it would be hard for him to stay with the group. If Grant saw a bird that interested him as they walked, he might just leave the group to go see it. The counselors had to work with him on this.

Grant also confided that he did not want to walk with the group. He wanted to walk alone with one of the counselors. He related better to adults, and he liked getting special attention. He thought that if he just didn't get up to go when the group left and instead stayed behind, a counselor would have to go back for him and then walk with him alone.

The counselors felt this was important to work on. Their solution was to not wait for Grant if he hung behind like that, or if they needed to wait for him, they wouldn't talk to him. He had to learn the necessity of interacting with the group and not just with one counselor. If he didn't keep up with everyone, he'd have to walk to the next activity alone. It was a solution that didn't work right away, but over time it had a positive effect.

When Grant did interact with the other kids, it was initially very awkward. One time, as a boy was telling him a story, Grant started walking in circles. The other boy followed behind him, around and around, so he could finish what he was saying. Grant needed to be taught that even though he heard every word, the message he sent by walking in circles was that he wasn't interested in what the other person was saying, and that he was being disrespectful. He didn't know what his body language said—that his behavior was rude.

His counselors were charged with trying to help him figure all these things out. They would break them down in ways that Grant could remember. The trick was getting him to remind himself to be aware and tell himself, "I always have to remember to do this." That took time, and reinforcement.

They also worked with him on sensory integration. When you or I sit in a chair, we experience and integrate many different sensations at once without any effort at all. We feel pressure from the chair and our feet touching the floor, we hear the sounds and smell the smells around us, our eyes adjust to the light. Kids with Asperger's can't sort out all these sensations and experience them harmoniously. Each one stands out and calls attention away from a central focus. Often, these kids feel overloaded by all the sensations coming at them at once. The camp counselors work with them on strategies to help them adjust.

Camp lasted for eight weeks, and after that Grant had a couple of weeks off before school started. It gave us time to get some strategies in place for the new year. One of the best strategies we took away from that first summer was to give Grant two options to choose from, rather than letting his mind run all over the place with choices. For example, instead of asking him what he wanted for dinner, I would give him two dinner options to choose from. It was very clear-cut and helped him focus. We also talked to him about being flexible—not insisting that things could only go his way. That one is an ongoing challenge, but we're working on it.

Grant did so well at YouthCare, we sent him back the next summer. After camp was over that year, the administrators recommended to me that I hire one of Grant's counselors to work with him and us privately during the school year. They knew that when Grant got into fourth grade, he'd have more homework than he'd ever had before, and it was going to be difficult for him to juggle if he didn't have help with focusing, expectations, and time management. Also, having someone who worked so closely with Grant at camp come and work in our house for an hour a week would help to reinforce the lessons from camp. It would help Grant to keep learning, and to continue to develop his social skills and focusing ability consistently throughout the year. We hired a counselor named Christina Lazdowsky, a graduate student, who would help Grant at home.

Going into the fall after Grant's first YouthCare summer, it was impossible for me not to think about the distance that both Grant and I had traveled in just a year. Twelve months earlier I could barely string together a sentence that had the word *Asperger's* in it without breaking down. (Okay, that was still more or less true eight months earlier, too—but I was improving!) Now I was entering the school year cautiously optimistic about applying all that Grant had learned over the summer and building on his successes.

——◆——

WITH GRANT AT CAMP for the better part of the day during the summer of 2008, I was able to focus a bit more on Gehrig. The beginning of the process was exhausting. I couldn't imagine what made a kid—a boy—stop eating. Curt blamed me for always worrying about what I looked like, and I blamed the media for always focusing so much attention on Curt's weight. Either way, between the media and me, I felt there was plenty of blame to go around.

Through the therapy, it came out that Gehrig didn't have body image issues—he was using food as a way to exert control in his life, the same way that he was getting rid of his Adderall pills in an effort to be in control. I referred to his outpatient program as Gehrig's summer camp that year. He went to therapy, we went to parents' therapy, and we all went together.

Was it easy walking into a room with parents who knew who we were? I didn't care. All I cared about was getting my son healthy. Gehrig was gray and thin. He'd been falling asleep in class during the school year. And he had been distancing himself from his friends. You see, having friends at that age would force him into eating situations. Not having a social life solved that problem.

I don't think we will ever fully understand why Gehrig starved himself. The summer of 2008 was a long summer. A child with an eating disorder will try to control how long he can outwait you. I spent many, many hours sitting at a table with him, not letting him leave until he ate enough. The dogs had to be put away during mealtime, so Gehrig couldn't quietly feed his food to them. And he wasn't allowed to go to the bathroom then, either. I went through this three meals a day, with shakes in between. I dreaded it because I knew I was stuck to the chair until Gehrig decided he was done fighting me. It could take over an hour to eat lunch.

One day that summer, Gehrig and I were talking, and seemingly out of nowhere he asked me bluntly, "Do you stay with Dad because of us kids?"

I didn't know what to say. I was speechless, so he continued. "Why can't you and Dad be like normal parents and do what normal parents do?"

It didn't take much thinking on my part to figure out what he meant by "normal" parents. Sure, he wanted us to have dinner and be friends with other parents, but probably most of all he wanted to see us together. He wanted us to go on dates and hug each other. He was right. Even though Curt and I loved each other, we had let our lives become a routine.

At the end of Gehrig's outpatient "summer camp," his counselor called us in. "I think the two of you should talk to someone, a therapist," she suggested. "You need help communicating. You need to do it for yourselves, and for your kids."

Curt and I had lived our lives essentially apart for so long, now that he was home all the time we didn't know how to live together and get along. I expected him to automatically know how to do everything I'd been doing on my own for so many years. It made me angry when he tried to do things his own way. We seemed to always be angry at each other.

On top of that, the counselor informed us that the divorce rate among parents of children with special needs is higher as the parents turn on each other under the stress of the situation. Neither of us was willing to let that happen.

"Would you take us on?" we begged the counselor. She happily agreed.

And so that was how the summer came to a close. Instead of August screeching to a halt with a stressful playoff race looming, it ended with a different kind of victory. A year later, in 2009, Gehrig entered his ninth-grade year weighing 115. He'd gained almost forty pounds in a year. Even though he didn't feel he could celebrate, we were proud of him for what he'd overcome. Meanwhile, once a week, Curt and I headed to therapy, as we tried to remember why we'd started this wonderful mess of a family in the first place.

ten

Making a (Flexible) Plan

OUR JOB AS PARENTS IS TO PREPARE OUR KIDS FOR WHAT IS ahead of them, to teach them the difference between right and wrong and how to choose wisely. Sometimes, especially in the case of a child with Asperger's, that's easier said than done. It takes parenting up to a whole other level.

After Grant's summer at YouthCare, I realized I needed to play a more active role in making sure he got the special services he needed, in and out of school. Grant was about to enter third grade, and while I had met with people at Grant's school on a few occasions during the first school year after he was diagnosed, I still had a hard time wrapping my head around the scope of what was required for him not only to excel, which we knew he could and would do in certain areas, but to survive socially in the classroom on a day-to-day basis. That said, each time I went in, I felt a little bit better prepared and more cognizant of what they were talking about.

What I didn't realize that first year but learned through YouthCare was that meeting with Grant's teachers wasn't just your run-of-the-mill parent-teacher conference but with more people; this was about tailoring services to meet Grant's needs. It was a complex and layered problem that would need to be readdressed and revised—not just throughout the year but throughout his education and ultimately throughout his life. We would have to keep coming up with different life plans for Grant at different stages, because two years down the road, the plan we put into place for third grade would no longer work for him. That fall we began a routine with the school that we keep in place today, revisiting his plan every six months, unless his plan isn't working out for him, in which case we can meet sooner to discuss his needs.

I have to admit that when I sat down for that first meeting at the school after Grant's diagnosis, I had no idea what went into getting services for a child. I had no clue about the protocol or what I even wanted to see him getting. This was my first experience with Asperger's, while Grant's teachers and the school administrators had dealt with this before, so I decided to sit back, listen, and hope they would guide me with nothing more than the best intentions for a great education for Grant.

As we sat down to plan things out for Grant in the fall of 2008, we looked specifically at how Grant had dealt with the school environment. A big part of how the school administrators and I plan for Grant is that we pay close attention to the specifics of Grant's personality. Though kids with Asperger's share certain traits, there is a lot of variation among them, and one of the biggest sources of variation is in how they deal with school. What we found as we looked over Grant's first school year since the diagnosis was that he had still managed to perform well. The good news for Grant was that because he is bright, his disability didn't interfere with his ability to be a good student. The bad news was that it did affect his ability to get the most out of school.

To help me understand, they showed me the charts they used to determine a child's needs. Using one chart, they considered how much the child's disability affected one or more of his or her life activities in and around school. For Grant, two factors were having an impact on his activities: having ADHD and having Asperger's.

Two of Grant's greatest difficulties were completing work and following directions. Those were due in large part to his ADHD. His trouble with maintaining adequate space and being easily agitated by changes in schedule were both due to his Asperger's.

To help Grant with his anxiety around shifts in his schedule, Mrs. Trikulous, who would be Grant's teacher that year, devised a strategy: She would make up a laminated schedule for each day of the week—five altogether—which would help to keep Grant on task.

From the start of the school year, this proved effective at keeping Grant focused and in control. She began referring to him as her "official timekeeper" because he was so hypervigilant about staying on schedule. If reading ran over its allotted time slot, he'd raise his hand.

"Mrs. Trikulous," he'd say, "we're still doing reading now, but we were supposed to be done with that five minutes ago and go on to math."

"Thank you, Grant," she'd say. "But it's okay."

Our meeting before third grade also determined that Grant required frequent movement breaks throughout the day, and during those breaks he would usually seek out sensory stimulation. Grant also had to start participating in more social activities during lunch that encouraged him to respond to limits and engage in activities with other kids. In the classroom, Grant's teachers would provide him with graphic organizing tools for writing assignments and allow him to take his tests in a quiet setting separate from the classroom, if needed.

While the meeting dealt with these specific techniques for managing Grant's day-to-day classroom behavior, it also focused on the programs the school offered outside the classroom. As mentioned earlier, there are two types of programs for kids with Asperger's and other disabilities: an Independent Education Plan (IEP) and a 504. Both allow kids like Grant to get special services in school, but the 504 is the less extreme of the two. It allows for them to have certain modifications and accommodations throughout the day, while an IEP provides for a more tailored education, including more time outside the classroom in special teaching environments, tests that are untimed, and other variations from the regular classroom experience.

During our first meeting in 2007, it was determined that Grant only needed a 504, and a year later, in 2008, we reaffirmed that decision. As part of that program, he met with a counselor once a week for thirty minutes to work on his social skills. The help he got each week with his social skills made it easier for him to understand appropriate behaviors. Sometimes those thirty minutes were spent on his lunch activities, where he'd learn to communicate with and respect others at the table. Other times they were one-on-one with the counselor. The goal was to help Grant understand when to talk, when to stop talking, and that it was rude to dominate the conversation.

Grant would also meet with an occupational therapist once a week to address his sensory issues. This work would help with both his ADHD and his Asperger's. As I listened to the school administrators talking about it, I was amazed at how seemingly simple—yet totally effective—some of the therapies were. One small tactic could begin a chain reaction that would result in a more attuned and attentive Grant. For example, merely placing a weighted beanbag in his lap could calm him. Providing him with that small amount of pressure helped him integrate all the sensations he was experiencing, and with calmer nerves, it was easier for him to focus in class.

The 504 plan also would provide a "sensory diet" in the classroom. The occupational therapist would use an example of an engine to help Grant know what level of energy was appropriate for different situations. She'd ask the question "How does the engine run . . ." and then fill in a specific setting or situation such as " . . . in class?" The goal would be to help him figure out that there are times when the engine needs to be quiet and listen, and then there are times, like recess, when it can run high. She would work on cues to help redirect him and would check in with him often, but she would also be careful to give him his own space when he needed it. Overall she would remind Grant of specific expectations, presenting her directions in a simple manner, both verbally and visually.

Of course, just as in 2007, it was hard not to be concerned about him socially, but as the school year began, it didn't seem to be a problem. He felt that he had lots of friends at school. Still, I worried about what the kids thought of him.

———•———

WHILE THE SCHOOL WAS taking tremendous steps to help Grant, the best thing I did for him was to hire Christina, one of his camp counselors, the following year, to come and work with us once a week for an hour. From the start, Christina provided us with helpful exercises and strategies that we could use daily to help Grant work on all of his issues.

The kinds of strategies she devised for his schoolwork were incredibly beneficial, and they weren't all big changes—they were actually a lot of small things. For instance, when most children are given one of those sheets with multiplication tables and questions, they find the tables useful and go about answering the questions. When Grant was given them, he shut down completely. It was just way too much information for him to digest. Instead, Christina suggested we try flash cards. With those, Grant was able to process one math problem at a time, and because it was more manageable for him, he became more comfortable. As it turned out, this sense of being overwhelmed also had a lot to do with Grant's anxiety over homework. Following Christina's lead, we started breaking his assignments down, and with those smaller doses, things began to feel more manageable.

Sometimes her solutions were as simple as a change of venue. Grant was better at speaking than writing and had problems getting his thoughts down on paper. Christina suggested he'd do better on the computer, which had increased his ability to focus in the past. Once he started practicing his spelling words on the computer, almost immediately the whole process went much more smoothly.

While school was part of what Christina covered with Grant, she would also help with his social issues. One of the most useful tools she gave us was a "social consequences map." On it there are four columns: (1) my action, (2) how I felt, (3) how others felt, and (4) consequences. She taught us to use this map whenever Grant acted inappropriately so that he could get a broader picture of the consequences for himself and everyone else.

The first time we used the social consequences map was after Grant's second sleepover with a friend at our house. His first sleepover, with a boy from his class named David, had been a disaster. Grant cried the whole time he was at our house. The problem was that they wanted to play different things, and they didn't have many shared interests. If David wanted to play a game that Grant didn't like, Grant would become frustrated by his inability to resolve it, then wander off and cry. He just couldn't grasp how to handle the situation. David would leave the room from time to time and go play with Garrison. Grant was at a complete loss about how to relate to David, and he didn't know how to handle the transitions from one thing they might play to another. He didn't understand about taking turns, doing what each person prefers, or that when you have a guest over, you make them feel welcome by doing some of the things they want to do.

Because of the problems with this first sleepover, we were reluctant to try it again with just anyone. If Grant was going to try once more, we knew it had to be with a friend he really got along with. Eventually we arranged his second sleepover with a boy named Mark, whom Grant just loved. He and Mark had much more in common, and they played together the whole evening—board games, video games, jumping on the trampoline. It was going so well that I was heartened. After the sleepover with David, I'd had this awful feeling that Grant would never be able to relate to other kids and never have close friends.

But my good feeling was abruptly interrupted on the second day. Grant brought Mark outside and told him it was okay to walk on the pool cover. Grant knew he was not supposed to do that—we had told him a million times. Mark didn't want to do it, but Grant kept telling him to, over and over. Finally Mark gave in. When I came out, I found Mark's pants wet, from the pool cover. Mark told me the whole story.

I had to yell at Grant, even though I didn't want to. I didn't want this nice kid who played so well with Grant to hear me yelling at my son. I was afraid it would put an end to their friendship.

The next week, when Christina came to the house, I told her about it. That's when she suggested the social consequences map. I sat down with Grant, and we filled in the columns, with Grant's action, how he felt doing it, how Mark might have felt, and what the potential social consequences might be. The answer to the fourth one didn't jump right out at him. Christina said I should also give him my impressions of what belonged in each of the columns.

"Grant," I said, "I think the social consequences here are that Mark might be mad. And your mom might be mad. And you might not be able to have sleepovers with Mark again. Do you want that to happen?" He shook his head no. The more we used that chart, the more Grant became aware of the impact his actions could have.

From the beginning it was clear that working with Christina was not just about Grant learning, it was about me learning as well. It was about having her coach me through my interactions with Grant and giving me tons of feedback about how I handled situations. Every week Christina would give me summaries to support what we had done with her during our session. For example, a sheet she gave me not long ago referred back to a difficult transition with Grant when she was at our house. He had been reading, and I told him I wanted him to take Christina upstairs and show her his room, where we had just put up his homework charts on the wall. Grant didn't want to move. He wanted to just keep reading. When I pushed him on it, he got upset.

On the sheet Christina sent me, she wrote: "With the transition today: 1.

I first would have told Grant he has five minutes to keep reading before we go upstairs to check out his room. 2. Give him a one-minute warning, and when the time is up, tell him we are going upstairs to check out his room, and then get his homework done. Obviously, the ultimate goal is that he will get up. 3. I think the more you begin to use transition previewing and time scheduling, the easier the transitions will become. Are you still interested in the daily schedule with him? I think it would be a fun activity for him to decorate a whiteboard and create his own schedule/icons, etc. If you want, I can get some of the materials and create a 'model' schedule."

———•———

BETWEEN CHRISTINA AND THE teachers at school, I quickly started to amass a list of tactics to rein in Grant's behavior. While they don't always work, and some work better than others, by and large they have worked wonders. Here are some of the strategies I've learned for helping Grant, from the people at his school, from his camp counselors, from the AANE, from his neurologist, and from my own experience. It's sort of my Asperger's cheat sheet, and I've found it pretty helpful. I share these with the understanding that every Asperger's child is different, and what works for one won't necessarily work for another, but hopefully some of these tricks will help others:

- Preparation: Before we go into new situations, I talk to Grant about what he can expect from the experience and what I expect from him in terms of behavior. This was the tactic I used in the final game of the 2007 World Series. I explained to Grant about the timeline of events ahead of us, about what we were doing there, and about the noises he would be exposed to. It worked like a charm.
- Two Choices: Rather than asking Grant broad questions like "What do you want for dinner?" and "What game do you want to play?" I give him only two options to choose from. It helps him engage and decide.

- Observation: When I go out in public with the kids, I keep an especially close eye on Grant because he is given to getting distracted and then wandering away.

- Don't Fight Everything: Picking and choosing my battles with Grant helps me maintain my sanity. Grant will try to debate with me and negotiate over every little thing. I no longer waste my time on arguments over the color of the sky, but I dig my heels in when safety is an issue.

- Look Me in the Eye: When I need to make sure that Grant is listening to me, I insist that he look me in the eye. Even though I know that makes him uncomfortable, it's the only way I can be sure he is paying attention to what I am saying. I will not let him go on until he makes eye contact.

- Reaction Scale: I use Brenda Dater's scale of one to five when I feel Grant is overreacting. If he is screaming and crying because he doesn't want to do his homework, or because we ran out of his favorite cereal, Trix, I will ask him, "Do you think a level-five reaction is appropriate here? Five is like a call to 911 because your house is on fire." That lets him know he needs to bring it down, big-time.

- No Body Slams: When Grant expresses his anger by running and slamming his body into me, I tell him, "Please get out of my space," and that when he can speak to me instead, I'm here for him.

- The Palm Rub: When Grant is upset, I rub the palm of his hand. This has a very soothing effect on him. He recognizes how helpful this is. When he is tired or just can't get his thoughts in order, he will put his hand out for me to rub.

- Upcoming Appointments: When Grant has sports practices or parties or Cub Scouts, I start telling him about those appointments days in advance. It helps me get him out the door. He doesn't adjust well if a practice is called off or a party is canceled, but hopefully we'll figure out a strategy for dealing with that one of these days.

- The Right Time to Talk: When most kids do something wrong, it's advisable to talk to them about it at that moment, while it's still fresh. With Grant, that doesn't work. I often have to wait—sometimes days. And then I have to present it to him first. I'll say, "Grant, can I have five minutes to talk to you?" Then he's more likely to listen when I go through how he could have reacted differently.

- Social Consequences Map: I use the social consequences map, mentioned above. Little by little, it's opening his mind to the consequences of his actions.

- Grant's Choice: I will sometimes let Grant choose the dinner a few nights a week, with the agreement that he then has to eat what others choose, the other nights. I also take deep breaths at dinner, and try not to lose my temper when and if Grant gives me a hard time about what's being served—sometimes even if he chose it.

- The Power of Routine: I provide the comfort of structure and routine. Grant appreciates getting up at the same time every day and following the same routine to get ready for school. I try my best not to vary that, and it helps him stay calm and focused.

Regardless of their effectiveness, these tips gave me back something I hadn't had in a long time: control. The more strategic information I learned about dealing with Grant, the more I began to feel that it was possible to parent my way through Grant's behavior. It wasn't easy, and perhaps the hardest parts were the things that went against my natural instincts as a parent. Fighting off those parental reflexes was difficult but essential.

I just kept telling myself that Grant's brain was wired differently, and in order for these tactics to work, I'd have to do some rewiring on myself.

eleven
Confessions of an Overloaded Mom

THOUGH THE TACTICS AND STRATEGIES I'VE DESCRIBED
changed the way I dealt with Grant, there was one thing they couldn't help
with: the unpredictability of life. As much as I tried to prepare Grant for everything, to get him ready, to give him the tools he needed to feel comfortable,
there were some things I just could not control. It was a hard lesson to learn,
and I have Halloween 2008 to thank for teaching it to me.

Being a very organized catalog and Web site shopper (who with four kids
has time to do all their shopping in person?), I ordered everyone's costumes
weeks in advance. The catalogs arrived in August, so the kids had plenty of
time to pick. I made sure the costumes were at the house early, and I hid them
from the youngest kids, who would otherwise wear them every day, rendering
them threadbare by the time Halloween rolled around. One by one, the pack-
ages were delivered to the house. Except for one. It felt like some horrible
cosmic joke: Grant's costume was the only one that never arrived.

He'd planned to be an American Indian. He'd been learning about Indi-
ans and Pilgrims in school, like most Massachusetts kids do each fall. There

is so much history here, and Grant was enthralled with what he was learning. He got completely pulled into the subject, learning everything he could, which inspired his choice of costume. So I went online and ordered it for him.

I waited and waited for it to arrive. The next thing I knew, it was the day before Halloween and Grant had no costume. In a panic I sent an e-mail out to local moms I knew, asking whether anyone had a spare costume. As luck would have it, no one did.

So the night before Halloween, I found myself driving around looking for an Indian costume for Grant. I didn't think I had much of a chance, but I tried. With a normal kid, I might have been able to switch gears and get him to agree to a different costume, saying, "Hey, this looks much cooler than an Indian costume!" But not a kid with Asperger's. Not Grant. He was locked in on that, the way he locks in on so many other things. To make matters worse, the school parade was the next day.

Before bed that night, I made a bargain with Grant. "Grant," I said, "if I have to make that costume myself, you will be an Indian." He smiled. "But can you please wear something different for the parade? If the costume comes in the mail while you're at school, I promise I'll run it over to you. And I promise you'll be trick-or-treating as an Indian."

I could see the wheels turning in his head. He seemed totally stuck and distressed. It's heartbreaking to see your kid in that state. Making this even more upsetting was that Halloween is one of Grant's favorite holidays. He often gets so excited that he has trouble sleeping the night before. He might fall asleep, but then he'll wake up way too early and not be able to fall back asleep.

Sure enough, I heard him padding around at 2:00 A.M. Curt and I took turns getting out of bed to tell him to get back in, hoping he could log a few more hours of sleep. He'd only had five, and that wouldn't be enough. At 6:30, when I was getting the older kids up, I found Grant in the living room, sitting on the couch. He was clearly exhausted. I told him to shut his eyes and I would wake him up when he had to leave.

This photo was taken at a crowded Chuck E. Cheese while we were still in Arizona. Grant was about two. Looking at this picture, I can vividly remember that the loud noise and commotion would cause him to shut down. Of course, back then I had no idea why.

Grant in 2001. Taking pictures of him was tough back then because if you asked him to smile, he would always say "No."

Grant with his younger brother, Garrison, in 2003. This was the year I started to notice big behavioral changes in Grant but passed them off because there was a new baby in the house. Still, we wouldn't have the official diagnosis of Asperger's for years to come.

This shot was taken in 2003 on Take Your Dad to School Day at Grant's preschool. Getting him to school that day was incredibly tough because it was a Saturday and he didn't want to go. He never went to school on Saturdays.

News trucks were crowded outside our house during Thanksgiving, 2003, as we negotiated with the Red Sox about Curt coming to Boston.

The day our family entered Red Sox nation (with Red Sox general manager Theo Epstein on the left and Red Sox owner Larry Lucchino on the right).

Every season the MLB teams would have a family day when the players' kids would get to play around at Fenway. This photo was taken during Family Day, 2004, our first season in Boston.

Curt with the kids in 2004 at the All-Star Game in Houston. It was the last All-Star Game he played in. (*Clockwise from top right*) Gehrig, Garrison, Grant, and Gabby.

Traveling with the kids during the season was always tough because it was usually just me or me and my mom with all four kids. Airport play places like this one were helpful, but the downside was that Grant couldn't understand when I said we had to leave. Many times we almost missed our flight because I couldn't get him to stop playing, he would not listen, or he would run from me.

This photo of me with Grant (*left*) and Garrison (*right*) was taken in 2004. Even though Curt helped the Red Sox win the World Series that year, Grant was probably the only person in New England who didn't pay attention. No matter what I tried, I couldn't get him interested in baseball.

A family trip to Disney World in 2005. Because Grant had a tendency to wander off without thinking, it was easiest for me to dress all the kids alike so that we could keep track of them in the crowds.

Grant and Garrison eating corndogs. As Garrison got older, it emphasized the differences between him and Grant, showing just how developmentally out of step Grant was in some ways. Grant also would lock into one food—this particular summer it was corndogs. Corndogs for breakfast, lunch, and dinner.

Since Curt and I were some of the oldest parents on the Red Sox, Family Day always meant that there were a lot of kids younger than Grant running around, which he loved. This was Family Day, 2005, when each of the boys had yellow hair gel to imitate Curt, who had recently let Kevin Millar cut and dye his hair during a rain delay.

Curt and Grant at Family Day, 2005.

Our kids quickly came to love Family Day because it gave them a chance to go out and play with their dad on the baseball field

This photo of Grant and me was taken at a Patriots game in 2005. Even though sports were mostly just background noise for him, it was a special day for Grant—just him, with no siblings around.

Grant was great when he first started playing soccer, but it didn't take long for him to lose focus. His behavior on the field was exactly like his behavior everywhere else: One second he'd be fully engaged, the next he'd be off in his own world. Until the diagnosis, these kinds of contradictions were really hard to make sense of.

Grant with his friends Patrick (*right*) and William (*left*) on the first day of kindergarten. Though Spinal Muscular Atrophy has kept William in a wheelchair for as long as Grant has known him, Grant has always shown amazing tenderness and awareness toward his friend's condition.

Christmas, 2006: Just like every other kid, Grant goes nuts for Christmas. Every Christmas Eve, after church, we rush home to see if the kids were good enough all year for the elves to leave pj's. If they did, everyone puts them on and goes to bed because Santa is on his way.

Grant, Garrison, and me at the Red Sox annual Picnic in the Park fundraiser at Fenway Park in 2007.

The summer of 2007 was the summer when everything changed, and Grant's ill-fated turn at Pop Warner football had a lot to do with that. Curt and I thought that the structure of football would be good for him, but all it did was show me just how wrong things were.

Our last Family Day, in 2007.

Everyone together after the Red Sox won the World Series in the fall of 2007. It had only been a few short weeks since Grant's Asperger's diagnosis, but I desperately wanted Grant to be there when the Red Sox won. I prepared him as well as I could, using some of the basic things I'd learned about Asperger's from the neurologist who had diagnosed him.

Grant playing Little League with his friend Stephen, who has Down syndrome.

It's tough playing baseball when you're the son of a professional baseball player (you wouldn't believe some of the things parents say in the stands), but it's even harder for Grant, who has always struggled to enjoy the sport. Since the diagnosis, it's become easier to focus him, but he doesn't always stay focused. Still, that doesn't mean other people really understand him.

Halloween 2008 taught me that it doesn't matter how comfortable you get with your child's Asperger's, life will find a way to complicate things. When Grant's Native American costume didn't show up, he was inconsolable. Whereas another child might have been flexible, an Asperger's child simply isn't wired that way. Luckily, my Medfield moms were able to come through in a pinch and find a substitute.

Grant's ninth birthday, fall 2008. His birthday always fell during the baseball playoffs, but because Curt was injured that year Grant was able to really enjoy his birthday with his dad.

For a long time Curt was looking for something he could connect with Grant on. They both found that something in Cub Scouts, which brought them together like nothing else they'd done before. This photo was taken on their first overnight with the Cub Scouts.

This photo was taken in the spring of 2009. Part of Grant's Asperger's is that he immerses himself in subjects that he likes, learning as much about them as possible. For a while now he's been obsessed with sea life, and since he was young we always believed that he would grow up to be a marine biologist.

When Grant was first diagnosed, I was overwhelmed by fears, but my biggest fear was that his Asperger's would isolate him, making it hard to keep friends. YouthCare, his Asperger's summer camp where this photo of him (with his arms folded) was taken, erased all those worries. For the first time I felt optimistic that, with specific attention, he'd be able to learn acceptable social behaviors that would help him throughout life.

This photo of the kids and me was taken while a photographer was shooting us for the magazine *Women's World*.

Grant's tenth birthday.

Grant's Christmas card photo for 2009. Animals have a powerful, soothing affect on Asperger's kids. Having one in the photo with Grant kept him much calmer and made him much more agreeable. I wish I'd known that a couple of Christmases ago. (*Photograph by Passaretti Photography*)

I can't begin to explain how much I've learned about Grant and about myself in the years since his diagnosis. My marriage to Curt and my relationships with my other kids are stronger than ever thanks to Grant. (*Photograph by Passaretti Photography*)

While this might have seemed like a reasonable solution, I had over-looked one crucial thing: the importance of Grant's regular schedule. He had a very regimented routine in the morning, as was the case for the entire day. He gets up at 7:00, gets himself ready for school by doing things in a particular order, and then goes to the "early school" session, which is kind of like a big recess before class starts. The kids love "early school," and Grant is usually there by 7:30.

Of course, it wasn't that I totally forgot about the significance of Grant's routine; as a parent you're always making compromises in one way or another. That day I thought the right call would be to sacrifice his routine for sleep. I figured there was more to be gained that day in giving Grant extra sleep than in adhering to his rigid schedule. Boy was I wrong.

I let him sleep an extra thirty minutes, and then tried waking him. But he wouldn't respond. He was that tired. After three failed attempts at getting him up, I decided his rest was more important than recess and let him sleep until 8:30. School was starting at 9:05.

When Grant woke up, the first thing that upset him was that there were different cartoons on television than he was used to. (Yes, even a shift in his cartoon lineup can lead to problems.) I was able to get him up and out, though, with a Star Wars Clone costume tucked into his backpack for the parade. But when we got to the school, instead of dropping him off out back as usual, I took him to the front. As I drove around to the entrance, Grant stiffened and started to yell.

"*Where are you going?!*" he shouted.

"School starts in five minutes," I said. "I can't take you in back where all the buses are now. You'll have to go in from here."

He kept yelling, "*What?! What?!*" all the while smacking his hands on the seat. It was clear to me that he was trying to get stimulation from some-where.

"Grant, this is where you're going to go in today," I explained again.

Suddenly tears were running down his face. I didn't know what to do with myself. I wanted to jump out of the car and run away. I wasn't expecting this, and I had no idea how to react. I knew I couldn't do what I might have done in the past—yell, *"Grant, get out of the car!"* No, my son was distraught, and it wasn't his fault. His schedule and his normal routine had been changed on him.

I remembered about rubbing his palm, and I took his hand and started to rub it. Slowly he settled down.

"We don't have to go in until you're ready," I told him. It took ten minutes to get him relaxed. Each second, I was afraid he'd fall apart again. He was that fragile.

When he finally pulled himself together, I asked him, "What was the biggest problem for you here?"

"I've never gone to school at this time," he said, "and I didn't know what to do."

My heart broke. That, in a nutshell, was what I was still struggling to understand about Asperger's. As much progress as I'd made, I still wasn't seeing the world through his eyes. Something as small as entering the building through a different door at a different time had caused him that much confusion and anxiety. What I naively thought would help him—letting him sleep late—had in fact messed him up. I was scared for him because I could feel his nerves and I had no idea what to do. I wanted someone to say to me, "Here is what you do in a situation like this." But there is no one-size-fits-all solution for these kinds of crises in Asperger's kids. All I could do was take a deep breath and pray that whatever I said would be right.

Grant dried his eyes with his sleeves and told me he was ready. Mrs. Trikulous was a gem. I had called the school to let them know what was going on and that Grant might be late. Mrs. Trikulous came and met us at the library entrance and then walked him to class.

I wanted to cry when I got back into the car. I couldn't believe what had happened. My intentions had been so good. I had only been out of bed a few hours, and already I was drained. And now I had to go and find a costume. I needed to have an Indian costume when Grant got home. I couldn't go through another event like this one.

Luckily I had planned to have lunch with a group of my girlfriends that day, and when I shared the story with them, like good friends and mothers, they all jumped into gear. One contributed feathers for a headdress. Another contributed face paint. Others offered jewelry, belts, shoes, and so on. By trick-or-treating time, I had the best little Indian costume you could ask for. We even temporarily dyed Grant's hair black. He looked great. Thank goodness for my mom and friends. Grant had a great Halloween. He liked being an Indian so much, he wanted to do the same thing the next year, and he did. Which certainly made my life easier!

What I was starting to learn, and what would ultimately prove just as important a skill as any of the tactics that Christina and the school would eventually teach me, was how to be adaptable. Sure, it's a parenting skill that I'd cultivated by dealing with my other kids, but Grant requires a level of adaptation that is far more intense. Simply put, adaptation is what has allowed me to parent my way through situations like Halloween 2008. It's the only real defense against the unpredictability of life.

Apparently adaptation was also something that my mom was learning when it came to Grant. Grant was Jack in a production of *Jack and the Beanstalk* at school, and it was very important to him that he make the character believable. He said he needed a brown poncho. He was very excited about being in this play, and also that they were videotaping it so he would have it for years to come.

I had a brown poncho and let him wear it on the day of the show. It went over beautifully, and Grant did a magnificent job. He knew all his lines and was totally comfortable and confident on stage. I felt so proud, watching him.

After the production, that poncho came home all balled up in his backpack, and I decided to send it to the dry cleaners. Two days later, Grant said to me, "You're not going to believe this, but the video recorder didn't work, so they're doing the play again tomorrow morning." Which was great—except that now the poncho, his top prop, was at the dry cleaners and we wouldn't be able to get it back in time.

He sobbed for at least an hour. I tried to come up with alternatives, searching the house for something else to use or to turn into a poncho. But Grant was beside himself. Curled up in the fetal position, he alternated between crying hysterically and staring off into space. I was seriously thinking this little prop hang-up might keep him from participating in the play. He couldn't figure out how he could do it without his poncho. He didn't want to feel this way, but he couldn't help himself. With any other kid you could say, "Pretend this is a brown poncho," but for Grant this change in a minor detail was essentially crippling. I had no solutions for him. We were both stuck.

At just the right moment, my mother called. "Mom, have you got any material I can sew together—a sheet or something?" I asked.

"I'll look," she said. "I must have something. I'll come right over."

About thirty minutes later, my mom showed up with some brown material. I took out my sewing machine and we got to work. We stood him up, sewed the arms, and cut a hole where his head would go. We purposely made the bottom jagged. Grant didn't like it at first, but after twenty minutes of convincing, he agreed that this was a much better poncho.

Later, after Grant went to bed, I asked my mom, "Where did you get that material?" I was expecting her to say it was an extra linen from one of her many moves. But no.

"It was the curtain from our spare bedroom," she said. She had torn a panel down just for Grant. Now *that* is a grandmother who understands Asperger's.

And here's the kicker: The teacher wound up running out of time the next day, so she had to postpone the taping of the play until that Friday. However, we were headed for Puerto Rico that day. Shockingly, Grant was a good sport about this.

"It's okay, Mom," he said.

I still haven't told my mom, though. I wonder how she'll feel about losing her curtain, considering that the poncho never got used.

———◆———

DESPITE ALL THE PROGRESS I was making, I was still struggling on a daily basis—not with Grant but with me. I was having an incredibly hard time keeping myself together. Dealing with Grant could be exhausting, but this was about much more than his behavior. This was about me and my behavior. This was about asking for help.

Curt and I had been going to couples therapy for a couple of months and we were making tremendous progress. For the first time in ages it felt like we were listening to each other better and communicating in a way that was totally different. In addition, Curt could see what I was going through every day with Grant. He was starting to view everything with eyes unclouded by baseball or distance, and it began to have a remarkable impact on how he acted around Grant.

While those were all very positive developments, they did not change the way I felt emotionally. During that fateful summer of 2007, just before Grant was diagnosed, I half-kiddingly predicted that either one or both of us would soon wind up on meds. In November of 2007, the second half of that prophecy had come true. I'd called our family doctor, who is also the kids' pediatrician, Dr. Shaughnessy, and told her I was ready for some help. I was tired of feeling angry and miserable so frequently. Too often I felt on the verge of ripping everyone's heads off. I didn't know whether my entrance into perimenopause might have played a role, but what did it matter? I was a wreck.

She prescribed Lexapro. I didn't ask questions. I assumed it was an anti-anxiety drug, but for all I knew she could have been giving me jelly beans. I didn't really care. As long as the pills offered just one bit of calming, I was ready to take them.

For so long, so many doctors—including Dr. Shaughnessy and going back to Dr. Rosenberger, who first diagnosed Grant's Asperger's—had recommended I get help. I kept mistaking their suggestions for insults, a sign they thought I was failing at my job of full-time stay-at-home mom and wife—the only jobs I had. My response, when I wasn't too offended to get an answer out, would be a very impatient "I don't have time."

The self-consciousness that I'd always felt as the wife of a ballplayer stretched to new heights following Grant's diagnosis. Though finding out the truth about Grant had been a huge relief when it came to the practical things and managing his behavior, it had torn me up internally. I was down on myself for all that was happening with the kids and their many diagnoses. I blamed myself for not noticing that Grant was really different and not getting him help sooner. I'd lie in bed at night unable to fall asleep because I couldn't stop thinking about all the times I'd treated him completely the opposite of the way I was supposed to treat him. The times when I'd yelled, the times when I'd punished—now that I understood more about how he processed the world, those scenes haunted me on a nightly basis. Instead of happy memories of Grant's childhood, the past seemed to hold only examples of my own parental ignorance.

While the medication helped me cope with all this, it did not solve everything. Over 2008, my intense scrutiny of myself had continued to snowball. I didn't cut myself any slack for playing the role of both parents much of the time, and for so long without the help of babysitters or a nanny. If I admitted to myself and the world that this hectic life was getting to me, that I was sad, would it seem I was ungrateful? I feared that was the case, so I resorted to acting. I tried to look as happy as people expected the wife of a successful professional athlete should look. My husband did something that millions of little boys dream of doing. We had plenty of money. I didn't have to have a job. I had four beautiful kids. What did I have to complain about?

On top of all that, I kept measuring myself against other parents. I looked around at other people's kids who were straight-A students and/or great athletes and felt like I was a failure as a parent—a failure at my favorite job, the one I took the most pride in. I was convinced that only the people who had parenting down could produce kids who were on the honor roll and the all-star team, the ones who were great at music or art. I clearly didn't have parenting down.

I thought about ways in which I had failed as a parent. In the summers, I took the kids to amusement parks, zoos, and on road trips instead of making them read and learn. Could that have messed them up? I wondered. I obsessed over this.

But worse than the comparisons I would make to other parents were the comparisons I made to my own mother. I knew that ideal I'd always held. I knew the kind of mother I'd wanted to be. And as I looked at the way my family was turning out, all I could see were my failings. My mother I was not.

I feared that the doctors who were telling me to get help knew my secret, that I was a lousy parent. In hindsight I realize that they were merely noticing how overwhelmed I was in my life, and how difficult it would be for anyone to handle the kinds of things I had dealt with for years—cancer, ADHD, anorexia, Asperger's, all the while being apart from my husband so much of the year, which had its own emotional challenges.

In the end, it wasn't anything specific that triggered my decision to seek therapy on my own. There was no rock bottom or eureka moment. Part of it was that the couples counseling with Curt had made me more comfortable with the idea of psychotherapy. Part of it was that I was just ready. But in September of 2008, I waved the white flag and finally called Dr. Shaughnessy for a referral to a psychotherapist.

"I need help," I said, my voice cracking a bit as I tried to hold back tears. She recommended Dr. Weather. I started therapy in January 2009, and I continue to go to this day.

Looking back, I don't know how I didn't know this, but I was depressed. I had thought the Lexapro was an antianxiety medication, but it turned out to be for depression. It's hard to believe I was unaware of it. I hid it from everyone, including me. I told myself that I never had time to be depressed, and that notion kept me busy and moving. I knew I was struggling with a lot, but I just kept smiling and trying to keep it a secret that I was really a mess inside. I convinced myself that I had it under control. For a long time I thought that if I admitted what was going on in my mind and asked for help, it would signal defeat for me. I had this idea that I had control over whether or not I got depressed, which couldn't have been further from the truth.

Looking back, I can see all the signs. If I had a day that had nothing on the calendar, which was rare, I would just sleep. I'd take the kids to school, do a surface clean of the house, and then escape from my world with all its anxieties by putting myself to sleep until the kids came home. I felt guilty for sleeping, and I think deep down I knew that it was a way of running away from my feelings. But it was my little secret.

I now realize that I'd been depressed for a long time. I look back, and it makes perfect sense. I would hear the noise of everything going on in the house, but I wouldn't react. I felt as if I were watching my crazy world from the vantage point of a fly on the wall. When I'd struggle with Grant, I would feel instantly tired or sick, and needed to lie down. He would badger me for things—like a bowl of cereal twenty minutes before dinnertime—and I would just look at him and say, "I don't care." And then I would crave sleep. Sometimes I thought I wanted to sleep until he was grown up.

My depression was big, and affected how I felt in every way. Sometimes I would convince myself that I had caught a bug, but really I had nothing contagious—just severe malaise. And my sleeping all day and catching "bugs" didn't happen frequently enough for anyone around me to put the pieces together and catch on to what was happening.

Even with therapy, I was still having difficulty asking for help at home. I was still trying to be the best mother and wife and not need too much. But I was struggling. After a few months of seeing Dr. Weather, she asked if Curt could come in for one of our sessions. I wasn't sure how he would feel about that. He questioned me about why she wanted him to come. I knew he was afraid she wanted to talk about him. But that wasn't the case. Rather, she brought him in to tell him that she was really worried about me. She did it in front of me, so I couldn't hide anymore. I needed help and I had trouble asking, so she asked for me. I had to accept that I needed others. For too many years, I had let fans' opinions mold the person I thought I should be and let other parents and society influence how I felt as a parent. I had been setting myself up for failure.

Curt was glad he came and agreed to take more of an active role with the kids at home. That session further improved the communication between us and helped me feel better about asking for help, whether from him or from other people.

Clearly therapy and Lexapro didn't make my problems simply vanish, but they did help me to become calmer and saner. I stopped staying up nights worrying about Grant and the past. Without the pressure of hiding my inner life, I started relaxing in ways that I hadn't in years. That in turn made me more patient (which is pretty necessary in a house full of ADHD). If I needed help, all I had to do was ask.

I gained a new perspective on my parenting, too. I realized I'd raised my kids the only way I knew—the way I had been raised. I was a happy kid. I turned out okay, I thought. My kids all played two sports a season and were learning to play musical instruments. Okay, they needed tutoring. But I was able to realize that I just wanted them to be kids and enjoy their childhood.

They didn't need to be the best at everything. They have their whole lives to figure out what they want to do and be.

Therapy and meds haven't "fixed" me or my problems. I handle it all better, but there's still a lot on my plate, and some of it can really get me down. Sometimes, when my depression gets the better of me and I start to feel alone, my therapist will prescribe something they don't carry at the pharmacy.

"Shonda," she'll say, "I think you need to make an appointment with your lunch bunch."

Don't get the wrong idea. My friends and I do not fit your typical ladies-who-lunch image. We do not get dressed up and go to fancy restaurants. In fact, we wear sweats and no makeup. The lunch bunch is sort of an unofficial support group made up of local friends. We get together now and then to let our hair down, take a break from our crazy lives, and just laugh about it all, together. We all need that now and then.

I had never had this experience until I landed in Medfield. I was probably cautious about making friends outside of baseball in the past because we moved too much, so I never felt I wanted to expose myself to people I might not be around for too long. It's not too easy to build a lifetime friendship with someone who might be gone the next week. Baseball is so transient, it's hard to let down your guard and find true friendship.

When we arrived in Medfield, though, I was somehow ready to broaden my horizons. The first person I met was Jen Ouimette. She had two kids in the same grades as Gehrig and Gabby. They ended up being on the same teams and in the same classes. Jen is vivacious and funny, and just happened to be from Maryland like me. We hit it off immediately. Jen made the move to Medfield easy for me. She let me know everything I needed to be doing with the kids. She also gave me a crash course in small-town involvement and introduced me to her friends, who, along with Jen and me, came to form the lunch bunch.

The lunch bunch has always been a godsend for me, but especially when I first learned of Grant's diagnosis. Even though I didn't want to talk about it too much, the group was there to hear what little I could get out, and to assure me that Grant would be okay. It's so nice to have a group of good women there for you in times of emotional need. Now that the kids are a little older and the subjects are changing, we tend to laugh more about some of the things that stress us out. You didn't hear it from me, but occasionally a story or two about a husband will find its way into the mix.

My mom, Jen, Ellen, Linda, and Heidi became a support system that I'd never had before. They have been with me right through my biggest struggles. After I've met with them, I always seem to walk away laughing and feeling better. No wonder my psychiatrist "prescribes" lunches with those women.

twelve
One Era Ends, Another Begins

AS I ATTENDED MY OWN THERAPY, I CONTINUED TO WORK with Curt in our joint therapy. It didn't take long for us to realize that entering marriage therapy had been a critical decision. Without realizing it, we'd started healing our relationship at an important juncture. Just as Grant forced us to rewire our parenting brains, we had to relearn our marriage from the ground up. While Grant had been part of what got us to this point, his situation revealed other fundamental issues that we needed to address.

With Curt injured and out of baseball for the 2008 season, there were a lot of questions that swirled around during the off-season about what he would do, and whether he was truly done with baseball. Over the years, this was something I'd thought about more times than I could count. Whenever things were tough with the kids or Grant was giving me a hard time, I'd find my mind drifting to a vision of what life would be like with my husband always around, being able to help in person and on the ground, not just remotely over the phone. For the wife of a baseball player, that idea of retirement sometimes becomes the Holy Grail of your marriage, an elusive date, never totally within your grasp, at which point you imagine that all your problems will suddenly evaporate.

While Curt wasn't officially retired after the 2008 season ended, having him around gave me a taste of what retirement might be like. And let me tell you, Holy Grail it was not. Oh sure, it was helpful to have an extra pair of hands around the house, especially with Grant, but it also revealed some of the differences that had grown between us, differences that had been heightened by all the emotional work we'd had to do with Grant over the last year and half.

Now that Curt was home, he was taking these sort of blind stabs at parenting that were only adding to the chaos. If Gehrig did something stupid—like telling his sister to get on the wrong school bus—Curt would yell at him and then level some huge punishment. "Okay, Gehrig, you can't use the computer for six months!" he'd say. Gehrig would get all upset. Then I'd come home and he'd tell me about it.

"Six months?" I'd ask Curt privately later. "*Six months? Are you serious? Don't you realize you can't enforce that?*" Then I'd have to go and fix things, and find a more appropriate, enforceable punishment.

I suppose it's to be expected that suddenly being under the same roof all the time would come with its own tensions, but it was harder adjusting to this new life than either of us had expected. Despite the struggles, in many respects it was perfect timing. It was incredibly useful to be experiencing these struggles while we had the therapy sessions to help us resolve the issues.

Still, just seeing Curt's face each and every morning and watching him fighting the battles, laughing with the kids, and pitching in when I needed him was wonderful. Sure, he had a learning curve to master with the kids—especially Grant—and I had to find patience for that, but I had confidence that in time we would get to where we needed to be as a couple and as a family.

By Christmas 2008, Curt still hadn't decided whether his life in baseball was over. His arm had healed and he felt physically better. On top of that, it bothered him that retiring now would mean going out on the disabled list. As the holidays inched closer, we spoke about it many times, but no decisions had to be made until the new year.

In the meantime, we continued to work hard on getting our family and our marriage together and happy. I think the whole family could feel that things were changing. The kids enjoyed having Dad around more. Even though we had always spent Christmases together with no baseball to interfere, this one felt different. Unlike before, this year we'd already had lots of time with Curt in the summer and fall. Christmas break from school didn't feel rushed.

It was especially nice to notice that Curt was more comfortable with Grant. He had gotten to spend more time with him and understood him better. He could even manage taking Grant shopping with him, which was a huge undertaking for anyone. Their time together was aided by the fact that Curt had been trying his hand at the video game business during his downtime that fall. Curt's company, 38 Studios, was developing a multiple-player online role-playing video game, and as it turned out, Grant was very interested. Suddenly Curt and Grant had things to talk about. At last, a topic of conversation he could lock in on with his father.

In the beginning of 2009, Curt began to work out a little to see how he felt. He worked out with a man named Eric Cresse, who was working with about fifteen to twenty young major league players. Curt wanted to see if he had it in him to keep pitching. He worked out long enough to know that he could, right up to the point where he had to either make a serious commitment to keep playing or retire.

As spring training began to inch closer, Curt and I both began to feel pressure about what he would decide. At a therapy session we were talking about what he was going to do and the various pros and cons of returning to baseball. Our therapist, Dr. Xavier, listened to us go back and forth, and then, almost out of the blue, she simply said, "You two have worked so hard to get where you are."

Her words stopped me in my tracks; she was absolutely right. Nothing was worth jeopardizing our progress as a couple and as a family. But what went unsaid, and what she and I both knew, was that this choice had to feel right in Curt's heart. As much as this was about our family, it was about baseball, too.

A few weeks later, Curt and I were trying out one of our new communication techniques at home: simply listening to each other. (It's amazing how much more smoothly a relationship works when you listen more.) We set some time aside, got a sitter, and went to a local restaurant to have a quiet meal and talk, just the two of us, with no one to interrupt.

We got into a discussion about the next baseball season, and right away he made it clear that he, too, knew that Dr. Xavier was right. The last two years had pushed us to the brink—both as parents and as people. As we spoke about it, it almost seemed as if Curt was relieved that I didn't really want him to go back for another season. I wanted us just to be a family. The kids and I needed and wanted him home.

Though we'd never actually said the words, everything we'd been working on had been building toward this decision. Curt had achieved a lot in baseball, and pretty much the only frustration he had to carry with him was the lack of resolution to his final season. But the more we talked through the situation, the clearer it was that the needs of his family outweighed his need to return for one final shot on the mound. He told me that what he was experiencing in his life off the field surpassed anything he'd ever experienced on the field. He didn't want to miss any more of life at home.

Then he said it out loud: "That's it—I'm retiring," and it was done.

The next day, with no cameras, no interviews, no fans, and no tears, he wrote a letter and posted it on his Web site, stating that as of that moment, he was officially retiring. It was March 2009. None of us have ever looked back.

In the end, the last game that Curt ever pitched was game two of the 2007 World Series. The day of the announcement didn't feel anything like I'd imagined it would. For years I had wondered when and under what circumstances Curt would retire. Whether he'd retire on his own terms or be forced out. You never know in baseball. I envisioned that when it happened, he would hold a press conference where he'd say good-bye to the fans and thank them. I would probably cry, since this was the only life I'd known for nearly twenty years. But none of that happened. There was no emotional farewell with a tipping of the cap to the crowd at Fenway followed by curtain calls and tearful postgame interviews—simply a post on the Web that made the day finally real.

No professional athlete ever makes the decision to retire based solely on his or her performance on the field, and no one in our family—not Grant, not Gehrig, nor I—was the reason Curt decided to retire. But as with any decision that affects your family, it's hard for family not to factor in. For nineteen years baseball had been the center of our world, the one thing above all else that could dictate the pace and the schedule of our lives. Now, at long last, we were making a different choice; we were choosing to put our family squarely in the middle. As we saw it, this choice was the most important thing we could do to hold it all together.

We were under no illusions that things would be perfect after Curt's retirement; lord knows that having Curt home during the summer of 2008 had eliminated those idealistic notions. But we did know that things would get better, not just because he was around but because for the first time in years we were listening to each other. And it was only by understanding each other better that we'd be able to truly help Grant.

———•———

AT THE BEGINNING OF 2009, before Curt had made his formal decision to retire, both YouthCare and the Asperger's Association of New England were planning their big galas, both of which were to be held in the spring. Each asked if we would attend.

Despite everything that had happened since Grant's diagnosis, I still had not spoken in public about Grant's Asperger's. It had taken me over a year to really open up about it—to myself and to others—but the experience with YouthCare camp had changed all that. It gave me the peace of mind and confidence that I needed to speak publicly about Asperger's. YouthCare had made me feel positive about Grant's future for the first time since his diagnosis. Whereas for so long I had struggled to envision what his future might look like, that summer, as I learned new ways to connect with Grant and build a more positive relationship, I also learned new ways of understanding how he would grow. This was all part of a long, ongoing journey, but at least now we were on the right path.

This newfound optimism made me feel as though I could finally begin to open up about what Curt and I had been through with Grant. So when both YouthCare and the AANE approached me, they managed to catch me at just the right time.

Becoming an advocate for Asperger's was something that had occurred to me before, but for a long time it was a role I was hesitant to take on. From my work with ALS and the SHADE Foundation, I had a sense of what being publicly associated with a cause would require both from me and from my family. Whereas both ALS and the SHADE Foundation were about my feelings, my experiences, and my desire to help, Asperger's was not as simple. This wasn't about just me; this was about Grant. Even if I'd been ready to talk about this right away (which I wasn't), there was no way I was going to risk talking in public about something my son was going through until I was certain that he understood this himself. In short, I needed to go through this as a normal mother, not as the wife of a famous baseball player.

However, my mind kept drifting back to that overwhelming sense of isolation I'd felt in the beginning. For so long I'd struggled on my own, keeping much of my fear and confusion bottled up. The more I thought about it, the more I came around to the realization that it was better for those of us struggling with this to be open with each other about it and to help other people become aware. There was comfort in community, and there were also strategies to be shared. Moreover, if I could help raise money so that other people could benefit from the kinds of services that were making such a difference in Grant's life and mine, then I wanted to take part in that.

I had come to feel tremendous gratitude for both the Asperger's Association and YouthCare. They were helping our family—and while things weren't quite running smoothly just yet, they were already more peaceful. In addition to the tips and information the Asperger's Association had provided, we also understood that there were people we could speak to about this, people who spoke from their own experience, who'd helped quell the sense of aloneness and the fears around having a child with these particular perplexing differences. Meanwhile, YouthCare was heaven-sent in its own way, a place where these kids with huge social issues could go and experience summer camp while learning strategies to help them not only now but later in life.

So when both organizations asked us to come, we really didn't have to think twice. We gladly marked the dates on our calendars. The more we thought about it, the more we realized how important it was to both of us that money be raised so that many more kids would be able to benefit from important, helpful programs. We decided to become cochairs for both events. One of my crazy faults is that I don't like to just put my name on things. Some people might look at that as an issue with control, but it also means that if an event has my name on it and it doesn't go well, I have only myself to blame. Still, it felt good to be part of these events. While I'd done plenty of charity work before, now that my son and our family were recipients of these organizations' services, I understood for the first time just how important it was to make them more available.

Being cochair comes with a set of responsibilities such as helping to get

auction items, finding sponsors, and inviting guests, and after a few meetings in preparation for the events, it occurred to me that I should talk about
Grant and what he'd been going through. It seemed funny to me that my
mind went there, because one of my initial apprehensions about hosting these
events was that I would be called upon to talk about Grant, and I didn't know
whether I should or could.

It wasn't a decision I could make on my own. I spoke to Curt and Grant
first to see how they felt about it. I knew that Grant understood about his
Asperger's and that it was what made him a little bit different. As he told a
fellow camper who was having problems one day, "Hey, do you know why
we're here? We both have some things to work on." (Leave it to Grant to come
up with the two sentences that pretty much sum everything up.)

Both Curt and Grant said that, yes, I could talk about Grant, so I committed myself to the speech, as hard as that was. Even though our friends
knew that Grant had Asperger's, it would be the first time we would talk publicly. For some reason I had the feeling that if I said the words out loud, I
would finally be okay with admitting that things in our house were different,
and that was okay.

A few days before the event, I sat down in front of the computer, and the
words just came to me. I had been holding in so many emotions, and they just
poured out. I had wanted to write about it before, but couldn't. I vividly
remember sitting down and trying just after the diagnosis, but I was too
numb, and my arms felt too heavy to write. I had way too much sadness to be
able to think straight. This time, though, I could write about where I was back
then. About how far I felt I'd come in a year and half. About what it was like
to be in a place where I was so overwhelmed, so frustrated, so confused, so
afraid, that when I sat down at the computer, all I could do was stare at the
computer cursor as it blinked on the white background. Now I could write
about how, when I finally opened my eyes to this experience, life became
much sweeter—how I can finally see the light, and it is beautiful.

It felt so good to write. I knew that I would be reaching people who were experiencing the kind of pain I had been through months before, when Grant was diagnosed. After I write a speech, my wonderful husband usually reads it, rereads it, and then adds to it. (I swear, he could have a second career as a writer or editor. He has a magical way with the English language.) I knew not to practice it out loud. I had learned from prior experiences that such emotionally potent material had to be read aloud for the first time in its intended arena. Not to mention that I wouldn't have been able to get through it without crying. The speech was emotional, funny, and thankful. When you speak from the heart you can never go wrong.

The YouthCare event came first. Many of the guests had no prior connection to Asperger's, but even so the event was beautiful and ran magnificently. When I gave my speech, I could feel the whole room respond. People were really moved, and they laughed in all the right spots, too, which made me feel good. As predicted, I wasn't able to get through it without crying, but I don't think anyone minded.

Curt spoke after me. He is very good off the cuff, or at least he was until he started explaining how funny some of Grant's behavior can be.

"My wife, Shonda, farted in a mall," he began. Immediately I wanted to die. "Grant turned to her and yelled, *'Hey, Mom, you farted!'* Most kids know better than to do that, but not kids with Asperger's."

I could have killed him. Although people appreciated having an opportunity to laugh. Looking back on it now, it is not so much the embarrassment that I remember, it's how perfect that story was. Sometimes I'll be going through things with Grant, and he will do something that so perfectly sums up what it means to have Asperger's that all I can do is laugh. The cause behind the event was a subject that was heavy, but this was a party.

At the end of the night, I noted how good and therapeutic it had felt to talk publicly about Grant's Asperger's. Our friends were supportive and let us know they were proud of us that night. They had also been on this journey with us, but that night I let them in more than ever before. You really don't ever know what's going on inside someone else's house.

I was set to give the next speech just ten days later, at the Asperger's Association event. The words were sort of the same, but the audience was different. This was an audience filled with people directly affected by Asperger's—either themselves or their children. In my speech, I talked about the struggles, the battles, how it was a different life than I had ever expected, but now the only life I would want. I almost got to the end of that one without crying, but then I started choking up.

Curt followed me again, this time with a Top Ten list: The Top Ten things you learn or experience with an Asperger's child:

10. It is humanly possible to say "Stop" four hundred times in a ten-second time frame.

9. You know the exact time you will be exhausted every day: within fifteen seconds of waking up your child with Asperger's.

8. At fifteen your Asperger's child will likely have an IQ twice as high as yours and let you know exactly when and how you were wrong every day.

7. Everyone at the grocery store, swimming pool, or other public gathering place knows your child's name, even if you didn't tell anyone.

6. Be prepared to never have the last word in any conversation ever.

5. Pray that if they have any nervous tics or habits, they don't include picking their nose.

4. Be prepared to be presented with more information than any human has the right to know about Legos, Star Wars, bulldogs, Bakugan, Pokémon, dinosaurs, Yu-Gi-Oh!, World of Warcraft, Webkinz, the human skin, bowel movements, and body hair—and hope your child only picks one.

3. Do not fart in public if you don't want everyone within earshot to know who, where, and what just happened.

2. Get ready for serious doses of unconditional love. The heart of an Asperger's child is not bound by society's norms, not limited to lessons we were told or taught, not confused or embarrassed by anything the heart emits. Theirs is a brand of unconditional love we should all pray at night to be exposed to, or to be able to extend ourselves.

1. Be prepared to go further than you dreamed, work harder than you thought possible, to love, and to cry, but at the end of the day wrap your arms around a true gift from God.

Once again it brought much-needed humor to the occasion, but as Curt spoke I noticed something else about him. Usually Curt and I hold hands when the other is speaking. It may seem silly, but it's our way of making each other feel supported and not alone with a little hand squeeze. As I listened to Curt give the speech, I noticed that he was becoming emotional.

This was one of the first times I'd seen him really react to Grant's situation and witnessed just how much this diagnosis had meant to him. Through everything—my therapy, our therapy, retirement—I'd spent a lot of time thinking about how my experience with Grant had changed me, but suddenly, at this incredibly public event, I was reminded of how much Curt's feelings had been affected. Watching him up there in front of the crowd, I saw that he, too, had struggled with his sense of himself as a parent. After all, this was the same man who'd idolized and revered his father—who'd put his father on a pedestal in the same way that I'd done with my mother. Just as Grant had forced me to look at myself in the mirror, he'd forced Curt to do the same. Curt is the most intense competitor I've ever known, and feeling like he doesn't measure up is not an emotion that he wears easily.

And yet here he was speaking candidly about Grant in this new life that we were living with baseball behind him. In a flash everything became dramatically real. Curt wouldn't be leaving for weeks at a time for much of the year anymore. He would see more and more how Grant reacted at home. This was his new reality, and telling the world about it made it really his.

What I didn't expect from the night was to have so many people thanking us for speaking. They told us that hearing our story was like listening to their own. As I was walking out the door, a woman was waiting to speak to me. She was young and teary-eyed. She was trying to say thank-you to me, but you could see that she was very fragile emotionally. It didn't take much for me to realize that this woman was where I'd been a year before. She felt alone, scared, and surrounded by people who didn't understand that Asperger's wasn't merely an excuse for bad behavior. She needed to know that she was not alone, that things would be okay, and that her child would have a prosperous future and friends. I listened to her fears and anxiety, and as her words slowed down, I found myself reaching to hug her, and saying the words that I had been unable to say to myself until a few months earlier: "Everything will be okay."

IN SPRING 2009 THE baseball season began, but now Curt was facing it in an entirely new way: as a Little League coach. For the first time, having just retired, Curt would have a chance to coach a kids' team.

I was curious about what kind of team he would put together, since he really didn't know the kids. His baseball season had always been during the kids' baseball and softball season, and that left very few games for him to attend. He and the other coaches had their "draft," and when he came home afterward, I asked to see his roster. I wanted to know the team had been assembled fairly. Some parent-coaches strategize about how to get the best team every year. I worried about what kind of team Curt would get, not knowing any of the kids.

I looked at the list. One name popped out.

"You know this kid," I said.

"Who's that?" he asked.

"He has Asperger's," I answered.

Curt turned that over for a quick second before elaborating. "At the meeting, people were yelling, 'We'll talk about him at the end of the draft. He's a handful.'"

In Curt's words, my biggest fears for Grant became a reality. They were probably talking about my son that way in another meeting. He very rarely gets the same coach from year to year, and I'm not surprised. One time an exasperated coach said about Grant, "His father's a Major League Baseball player and he doesn't even know how to hold a glove?!"

Part of it I understand. Grant is difficult. Kids like Grant can pose serious challenges on the field, where they can be on one minute and in their own world the next. It's especially hard on a coach who has never been exposed to kids who aren't typical. In light of this, it really was no surprise that the kid with Asperger's was avoided by everyone in Curt's draft but Curt. But it was still very upsetting, especially the things people said about him. I looked at Curt.

"That must be what they say about Grant," I said. I thought about how misunderstood he must be by people outside our little circle. You can tell people he has Asperger's, but a lot of the time people don't understand exactly what that is. And the bottom line is, they don't want him. I can't even begin to explain how bad it feels to realize your kid might not be wanted. It's humbling, to say the least, when you realize you can't protect your child from this kind of thinking.

Unfortunately, it wasn't long before I encountered this kind of attitude with Grant's coach directly. That same season, after Grant had been assigned to a team, I called Grant's coach to give him a heads-up about Grant's Asperger's.

"Ah," he said, "I figured it was something. I just didn't know what."

"Yeah," I said, "some days he'll be on, and other days he'll be off and it won't be so easy."

Well, not even three weeks into the season, I discovered that Grant would often sit in the dirt and play rather than take the field, or worse, bat, since he had been hit by pitches a few times. It was hard for me to come to the game to watch him dig in the dirt. I called one of Grant's camp counselors, Joelle, and asked for some advice.

"Don't let him quit!" she insisted. "Ride out the season. It will be good for him."

She offered to write a "social story" for him. It was a popular technique at YouthCare. She would write a story mapping out what was going to happen, like "On Tuesday, your team will be playing X other team . . ." The story would explain batting and fielding, how important it is to be a good teammate and stay alert. It was remarkable. The more he read it, the easier the game would be for him. He would understand the changes and be ready for all transitions.

Joelle also told me to ask the coach if he would mind doing one small thing: Instead of asking Grant if he wanted to play, to which Grant would say no every time, to give him a choice of two options. For instance, ask him whether he would like to bat fifth or eighth. The choice would be his to make—it would be on his terms, which would keep him engaged.

I called the coach and thanked him for coaching. "It's a big commitment," I said. Then I asked him if he would mind if I made a suggestion that I had learned from Grant's counselor. I told him what Joelle had said about giving Grant two options.

"Shonda," he said, "you know it isn't always about winning. I don't have a problem with a kid who comes here and tries. I do have a problem with a kid who doesn't try."

I don't think I could have been more stunned. The man clearly didn't get it. He didn't understand that if it seemed Grant wasn't trying, it wasn't because he didn't care, it was because he had certain neurological issues. To add insult to injury, the coach suggested that Grant played better when Curt was there. Once again I was back to defending my parenting and my choices about Grant's playing. Out of sheer shock, I said, "I am very shaken up and cry almost every day over these battles."

"There's no reason to be upset," he said. "He's a nice kid." I thanked him and hung up. So much for understanding.

———◆———

A FEW WEEKS LATER, CURT was interviewed on the radio. The host of the show asked him about the YouthCare event, and why he was involved.

"We have a child with Asperger's," he explained. "YouthCare is a great camp for Asperger's kids and their families."

He then told the story about the draft for the team he was coaching. He expressed anger over the way the other coaches tried not to get saddled with the Asperger's kid. His intention was to convey how sad it was to think that his own son could be looked at that way.

That night I had a Medfield baseball/softball board meeting. It was a board that had only one other woman on it besides me, and many men. There were about twelve men there that night with whom I'd worked closely over the past year to raise money for the baseball and softball fields at the local high school. You could feel the tension in the room. The board had made a decision with regard to Grant's friend Stephen, who has Down's syndrome: They decided it wasn't safe for Stephen to play anymore.

Listening to them debate, I felt partially responsible for this drama. Two years before, I was coaching softball and the opposing town had a player with Down's syndrome. It was beautiful and uplifting to watch her interact with the other girls, and the girls with her. That inspired me to reach out to Stephen's mother, Reka.

"Have you ever considered letting Stephen play baseball?" I asked.

"No, I haven't," she said.

I told her about that special little girl. I talked about how Grant played, and so did his other best friend, William, who suffered from spinal muscular atrophy and was in a wheelchair. William wasn't able to play the way the other kids did—the strength in his arms had been starting to weaken—but when the season was about to begin, they found a way for William to stay in the game: He would become the "assistant coach," in charge of the lineup. William is an avid baseball fan, and this was a perfect alternative for him that allowed him to be included.

Reka signed Stephen up then, and he was on the same team with Grant and William. When she went to sign Stephen up this year, she assumed the season would go the way it had last year. But now things were different. The league told Reka this year that it would be dangerous for Stephen to play and that maybe he should play on a special team for handicapped kids. She was devastated. I was, too, because I felt I had set her up for this heartache. Not to mention that the kids were still at an age where they weren't so likely to get hurt.

I talked to the person who had turned her away. I had known him for years, and he is a nice, nice man. He was upset about the decision but said it became an issue of liability. In talking to him, we both decided that maybe we should invite Reka and her husband, Nick, to a practice and let them decide whether it was too rough for their son. They agreed. I figured I should be observing a practice, too, to see whether Grant could get hurt.

I spoke at the board meeting and explained that Nick and Reka were going to watch a practice. "I assure you that Reka and Nick would never put their son in harm's way," I said. "And, by the way, since when did third grade baseball get so competitive that we can't find a spot for Stephen on the team? None of these kids will ever make it to the big time. I live with a major league player, and believe me, it's probably never going to happen. And if it is, this third grade season won't be the one that makes or breaks your nine-year-old."

I just couldn't believe people could be that serious about the success of their kids' team in the third grade. Wasn't it more important at this age to include someone like Stephen? I thought about all that the kids could learn from having him on the team. That was much more important, in my eyes, than winning.

I referred to Curt's draft experience. "I essentially have that kid you were all talking about," I said, my voice cracking. "I have a kid with Asperger's."

Well, I hit the hot button. I was screamed at by one man who started pointing his finger at me and saying, "I took that kid for two years, and I had other kids' parents consoling me for the way he acted and the way he spoke to me." Then more of them jumped in.

"I don't like the way Curt talked about our Little League on the radio," one said. "We do a good thing, and we don't deserve to be painted that way." It got ugly. Some people spoke to me more disrespectfully than I have ever been spoken to—and for something my husband said, no less. If you know Curt, he has had a lot to say over the years. But they aren't things that I've said, and I shouldn't be held accountable for them.

I was in shock and complete disbelief. I fought back tears in this room filled mostly with men. I knew that if I cried, it would be clear they'd gotten to me, and I didn't want to give them the satisfaction. They were so busy yelling at me for the way Curt had portrayed them, yet none of them had the guts or nerve to actually talk to Curt about this. But the truth is, I have been involved in kids' drafts for years, and it isn't just our town. There are coaches in every town who act this way.

"That is basically my kid you're talking about," I kept telling them.

I eventually had to walk out of the room. You know how sometimes, after a fight, you shake and cry a little? Well, I did both, *a lot*, in the bathroom. Being attacked without any ally to defend me was horrible.

Many of those men later apologized to me for some of the others, saying they were so shocked at their attacks on me that they felt frozen. To this day, the ones who went after me have not apologized. Nor have they ever had the guts to say anything to Curt about what he said on the radio. No, they came to me.

It's okay. I don't need their apologies. Their behavior was an inadvertent gift to me. Ever since Grant's diagnosis, I'd been living in fear about what other people were saying about him, about how they were judging him. While this meeting had confirmed all those fears in a painful and aggressive way, it was also a powerful wake-up call. It made me angry, but it also showed me just how much people needed to be educated about Asperger's. Suddenly what had begun with the Asperger's Association and YouthCare events became a mission. I refused to sit back and have people treat my son badly or speak negatively about him. I was going to become an advocate, for my son, and for others with Asperger's.

In the end, despite all the fighting and the bickering, there was a happy ending for Stephen and his parents. The board and Stephen's parents came to an agreement that Stephen wouldn't play on the field but that he would be the first batter up every inning. He would run the bases and it would never count. Stephen was thrilled. The kids and parents all cheered loudly every time he ran the bases. He smiled the whole way, and then his teammates would greet him at the fence to high-five him. It was thrilling and heartwarming to watch and be a part of that, and to see him included.

There, on the field, I realized that you can't tell kids how to be kind to people who are different. You have to show them.

thirteen
Like Father, Like Son

⁂

ONCE CURT HAD COMPLETELY COMMITTED HIMSELF TO RETIR-
ing, he was able to see what life was really like with Grant—full-time. When he
retired, Curt had a lot to walk off the field to. His oldest son was about to start
high school, his little girl suddenly looked like a teenager, Grant faced challenges
each and every day, and Garrison was already in the first grade and not a baby
anymore. It was a lot for him to digest and adjust to.

Suddenly Curt could see with his own eyes how Grant drained me and
would try to intervene, and sometimes he'd still yell, which I couldn't stand
for. I'd try to listen and let him handle it, learning for himself, for as long as I
could. But then that mother bear instinct would take over and I'd try to get
him to stop.

"Stop yelling at him!" I would shout at Curt. *"It doesn't work!"*

While Curt had been working with me to rewire our parenting skills for
months, it came as little surprise to both of us that I'd had more practice with
it. Though Curt had made tremendous progress with Grant through video
games, they still were not connecting on an emotional level.

Finally, one day after Curt and Grant had gone through a few frustrating exchanges, I simply told Curt, "You need to find something in common with Grant." As you can imagine, telling Curt how to parent went over real well. But the good news was that Curt realized there was something behind what I was saying. That was where the Cub Scouts came in.

I had suggested Cub Scouts because I thought it would expose Grant to great learning experiences with other kids, and it would also give Grant and Curt some special time together. There was a lot of interactive dad and son stuff, which might allow them to find common interests while giving Curt the chance to observe some of Grant's social tics.

In the beginning, things weren't exactly smooth. Grant's aversion to new things made Cub Scouts something of a tough sell, and while there were aspects that got him engaged and excited—campouts, sleepovers, getting badges—there were also more mundane things that just didn't grab him, so he'd space out instead. But regardless of his hesitation, Curt and I decided it was worth taking a chance. We pushed him into Cub Scouts and hoped for the best. We weren't let down.

It didn't take long for Curt and Grant to have some really nice bonding experiences through Cub Scouts. On their first overnight, they built their tent together, brought snacks, and did the whole campfire thing. It was freezing, and for some reason Curt had bought a sleeping bag that would have only fit Grant, so they had to share Grant's full-size bag and sleep together. It made me smile to know that Grant had had his dad's undivided attention for one day. That is not something Curt had done with anybody else in the family. Curt, for his part, came back beaming because Grant had been engaged the entire time and they'd had a blast together.

A few months later, they had a sleepover on the USS *Massachusetts*, a perfect opportunity for Curt to begin sharing his World War II obsession with Grant. They spent hours touring the ship, which was heaven for both father and son. They watched movies narrated by veterans who served during the war, and "racked out" on bunks about three feet too short for Curt. Grant's friend Stephen was part of the troop, too, and Grant made sure he shepherded Stephen all over the ship, explaining things as if he had actually sailed on it himself. He did get distracted by the news that there was ice cream coming, though, so until dinner and dessert Grant was pretty focused on making sure he didn't miss that.

As if Curt and Grant spending time together weren't a reward in itself, there was another positive result of their newfound connection: Not only would Curt help me in situations with Grant that typically devolved into battles, sometimes he even took over. For example, on Saturday mornings, when the kids had soccer, I used to wake up and pray that Grant would just put on his shoes and shin guards and get in the car, but eight times out of ten, it was a fight.

Suddenly with Curt around and involved, I had someone else helping to corral Grant and get him ready. He was there, right beside me, experiencing the kind of frustration I used to only report to him on the phone. Though it was hard to see Curt struggling just as I had, it was reassuring to know that the struggle was no longer entirely on my shoulders. All at once Curt had joined me in finding solutions that worked—and also in celebrating the good parts of Grant along with me.

As he spent more time with Grant and learned more about Asperger's, Curt grew more patient with him, eventually becoming the voice of reason in some situations. Whenever I'd get freaked out that Grant was still into Legos at the age of ten, Curt would look at me and say the thing that I'd needed to hear for years: "It's fine. Don't worry about it. I think it's great."

———•———

PERHAPS IN PART BECAUSE of the Cub Scouts and being outdoors, or because they are father and son, there was another area that pushed Curt and Grant closer together: their mutual love for animals.

The older Grant has gotten, the more his love for animals has been readily on display. If you ask Grant what he wants to be when he grows up, he'll tell you that he wants to be a veterinarian, and honestly I can't think of anything more fitting. He loves animals. He could watch *Animal Planet* all day, but more than that, he gets very attached to pets, and even to animals we don't know. He will sometimes disappear when we're out as a family if he sees a dog that draws his attention.

Kids with Asperger's tend to gravitate toward animals. They find something soothing about being around them, and it helps calm and focus them. Dr. Temple Grandin, the autistic author of such books as *Animals in Translation*, talks about kids on the autistic spectrum relating to animals because animals are similarly sense-oriented. Whatever the reason, Grant is no exception. When he's in the company of an animal, he's a different person.

Curt has always been into animals, so we've always had lots of creatures running around the house. When we first started dating he had two Rottweilers, and he's pretty much had animals around ever since. Me, I was never much of an animal person. I didn't grow up with pets, and I could really live without them. As far as I'm concerned, the Schillings have always had way too many animals. But Grant and Curt, on the other hand—they're a totally different story.

Grant has always loved having all the animals around. When he was four, we got him the first pet of his own—a hamster. As much as Grant loved his hamster, he wasn't the best at keeping it in its cage, and eventually it ran away. We should have learned our lesson from that one, but since we already had the cage in the attic, we gave Grant another hamster when he was seven, which he named Sox.

We figured that because he was a little older, he would be more careful when he opened the cage, but still he let the hamster get out of the cage a lot. This was before Grant was diagnosed with Asperger's and before I really understood how hard it was for him to avoid getting sidetracked. Looking back on it now, I can understand why he ended up losing his hamster a lot more than most kids do.

Usually, after it disappeared the hamster would show up within hours, or a day or so. But then, finally, the hamster seemed to be really gone. Day after day the little critter remained on the loose. After about a week, Curt and I figured it had either escaped from the house or died somewhere in the house, and we'd be smelling it soon.

We decided we needed to talk to Grant and tell him . . . something, we weren't sure what. We gave ourselves the night to think about it, after Grant went to sleep. Curt and I talked about it for a while, strategizing about the proper phrasing for Grant before finally going to bed. Then, at about two thirty in the morning, I woke up. I felt as if someone was poking a fork into my leg. I figured it was a dream, and tried to go back to sleep. After a minute or two, though, the poking started again. No, it wasn't a dream. It was a nightmare: The hamster was in our bed with us!

I started screaming, *"Curt! Curt, wake up!"*

I couldn't stand to turn the light on. I was completely grossed out by the thought of the hamster being in bed with us. I didn't want to see it.

"What's wrong?" said Curt, groggily.

"I think the hamster is in bed with us!" I shouted. He jumped up and turned on the light. Sure enough, there was Sox, sitting on my pillow, staring at us with this expression that said, "What, guys? Is there a problem?"

"You get it, Curt!" I yelled. I didn't want to touch that beady-eyed thing. Just as Curt reached over to grab him, he jumped away. For ten minutes we were chasing this little rodent around the room and laughing hysterically. I often think that hamster had to have had a death wish to jump into bed with me.

Sox hadn't been back in his cage two weeks before Grant begged me to let him take the hamster to the house of his friend who had one of Sox's sisters. It didn't sound like a good idea to me—it had trouble written all over it. I would never have agreed to it except that Grant's friend's parents, a wonderful couple named Maura and Dave, said it was okay.

"Okay, Grant," I said. "Just this once." I was nervous about it, to say the least. In my mind, having Grant over would be enough of a challenge for Maura and Dave. To have Grant with an animal in tow could only add a level of frustration.

The day of the big hamster playdate arrived. I dropped Grant off, and he was so excited he bounded out of the car. He was there for about two hours, and then I returned to pick him up. Maura came to the door, red and giggling. This is a woman who is usually pretty composed and serious. In the six years I have known her, I've never heard her utter a swear word or raise her voice.

She kept laughing. "I have to tell you something," she said, when she caught her breath, "and I don't know how to say it. It's kind of embarrassing."

My mind immediately started spinning from one image to another, as all I could think was, *Oh, my gosh, what did Grant do?*

"I was on the phone," Maura said, "and things had gotten very quiet, so I walked up to check on the boys," she said. "When I got there, I found them staring at the hamsters—who—" She started laughing again, and she looked at her hands, trying to figure out a way to use them to tell me what happened. "They were . . ." She was having a really hard time getting the words out. Finally, she took a deep breath and said, "The hamsters had just finished having sex."

To hear this very staid woman say "sex" set me off laughing.

"Grant looked at me with the straightest face and said, 'I'm mating them,'" she went on. "He told me they kissed, wrestled, and then went to opposite corners." I thought that sounded a little like marriage.

Grant's intention, it turned out, was to have hamster babies. He had read about hamster mating in a book and decided to put it to the test. He loved hamsters, he loved babies. Why bother with asking Mom and Dad for another one when you can make them yourself? That was the whole reason behind the hamster playdate.

Needless to say, all the parents had a big laugh over it. E-mails went back and forth, and we joked about visitation rights and hamster child support. For whatever reason, although I ultimately was not destined to be a hamster grammy, I did learn everything there was to know about hamster mating. Like, for instance, that it takes only fourteen days to produce a large litter of baby hammies. A hamster lesson and a great laugh, thanks to Grant.

Sadly, because of Grant's attachment to his animals, we've never been able to tell him when one of our animals passed away. We thought he would get too upset. Because Grant is so sensitive to begin with, he gets especially emotional where his animals are concerned, so when his hamster finally died, we talked Gabby into telling him it was hers that had passed away. Grant felt very sad about "Gabby's hamster" dying, and he made a sweet, genuine effort to comfort her.

The only problem was that every time Gabby got mad at Grant, she would use it against him. She'd say, "It was really *your* hamster that died!" and we would have to stare her down to make her take it back.

IT'S IRONIC THAT WE'VE had dogs, fish, lizards, turtles, and hamsters, and despite the fact that everyone but me seems to love all these animals, the job of caring for them ultimately falls to me. Without fail, whoever asked for each pet wouldn't uphold his or her responsibilities around feeding and cleaning up after the animal, and suddenly I would have a new job on top of all the other caretaking I was juggling. Every time, I wound up thinking, *I should have seen this coming.* I mean, we all know it's the mom who gets stuck with pet duties.

Somehow, though, I keep saying yes. The kids know how to get to me. They promise that this time they will *really* take care of the pet in question.

Really they will. They gang up on me. And Curt is just as a bad as the kids. I always fall victim to the one-husband-and-four-kids-against-me trick when it comes to adopting animals.

When our dog, Slider, died, Curt talked me into getting another one by saying, "We have to have a dog." It was the last thing I wanted, but Curt just kept at it. Like Grant, he can keep up a campaign until you give in just to shut him up. Finally, I caved and gave him another one for Christmas, which we named Patton. But one dog wouldn't be enough. After we had Patton for a year, everyone was concerned that he was lonely. And so we got Rufus, a shar-pei/pug mix.

You'd think two dogs would do it, but no. A couple of years ago, Gehrig and Gabby started begging us for dogs. Curt promised them both that when they got to be thirteen, and when he was retired, they could each get their own dog. Of course, he never consulted me about this. Curt is impulsive-ADHD-person-in-chief in our house. In the winter of 2009, Gabby started in on Curt again to get a dog. She was only eleven, but she had done all the homework on the Maltese. Of course, at that point Curt still hadn't officially retired, but he played the card that since he would probably be retiring, he would be able to help out with a new dog. (I swear, I actually have five children.) So we got Ellie, a Maltese. Then, in the spring, it wasn't fair that Gabby got hers before Gehrig got his, and we ended up with Georgia, the bulldog.

I now had four dogs. The kids' taking care of them lasted about a month. Gabby said to me, "I am so over it," and then rolled her eyes. They didn't want to clean up the poop and the pee. They couldn't be bothered with training. They wanted to cuddle their dogs and then let them go. As I suspected might happen, I became the main caretaker. For a while I thought the wet vac was an appendage of my body. I have become way better at spot cleaning than I ever thought I would need to be.

But when we weren't talking about stain removal, there was a lot of excitement about having two puppies. Of course, all this did was make Grant talk constantly about what dog *he* would get. Not surprisingly, he was relentless.

Like father, like son. More than anyone in the family, Grant and Curt were the true dog and animal lovers. Grant had an incredible sensitivity to them, and Curt was raised with them. Now that Curt was home, Grant was always talking to him about our pets, or telling Curt about the latest from *Funniest Animal Videos* or *When Sharks Attack*.

"When can I get a dog?" Grant asked a million times. When Grant gets it in his mind that he wants something, he'll beat you to death with it. I believe he could make the most hardened criminal confess after a few minutes.

I stood my ground. "No, way," I said. "Not now. When you're thirteen."

But Grant knew that Gabby hadn't needed to wait until she was thirteen. He knew there had to be some way around it. At the time, the buzz around the house was all about Gabby hitting her first grand slam in softball, and Grant put two and two together. As his last game of the season approached, he asked me, "If I hit a grand slam, can I have a dog?"

That agreement was actually tempting. Since Grant had all but quit batting, I thought this was a way to get him to really try—and there was very little chance he'd hit a grand slam, so we probably wouldn't have to get another dog. If he went to the plate and hit the ball pretty well, he would feel good about himself and it would inspire him. He could find out what he was capable of. That's how you build confidence, and confidence was what Grant needed. (Lord knows he didn't need a dog. Or, I should say, *I* didn't.) I made the deal, and the next week Grant went off to his game, prepared to hit a grand slam.

I was supposed to coach that night, but we'd recently started having Gehrig coach Grant as a way to build a better relationship between them, and Gehrig texted me throughout the game, letting me know how Grant was doing.

"He hit the ball really hard three times," Gehrig texted. I was thrilled. As I suspected, he didn't hit a grand slam. But what did it matter? He'd played better than ever before. I was excited about getting home to talk to him and find out how he felt about his night. I was prepared for a celebration. But that's not what I got, thanks to Asperger's.

Instead, I was greeted by a crying, inconsolable boy. Grant cried and cried for hours. He couldn't see that he'd done a great job and played his best—better than he ever had before. He could only see that he'd failed to hit a grand slam. He'd set a goal for himself and didn't achieve it; that was his singular focus. There was no budging him out of his narrow line of thinking. His heart was broken.

"Honey, I can't handle another dog right now anyway," I said. "But maybe we can get something else."

I really didn't want another rodent. Fish don't last very long in our house. But we had recently been to the pet store to pick up dog food, and Grant was completely taken with the birds.

"Can I have a bird?" he asked excitedly. *Sure, why not,* I thought. *How much trouble can a bird be?*

The last day of school, we went and got a bird. He had one in particular in mind. He picked it out, and we took it home. We named it Griffin—of course, a name beginning with *G*. Grant was so excited.

The next morning I woke up, and the bird was riding one of the dogs. After that it was pretty clear that Grant couldn't handle the bird himself. We moved it into Curt's office, and now it's everyone else's responsibility—which is to say, mostly mine. If you ask me, a bird is sort of a silly pet. You can't cuddle with it. But even though Grant and Griffin can't snuggle, Grant loves that bird and talks about it all the time. He takes a certain pride in it, which almost makes changing the newspaper in its cage worth it. It does make me feel good for him, though. Good enough to deal with the bird for twenty years, I'm not so sure, but that's how long they live. (I asked.)

I have no idea how long we'll be able to go before Grant resumes hounding us for a dog. Curt has been talking about not making him wait until he's thirteen because he already shows a lot of mature concern for the dogs, always reminding us to feed them and give them water. That makes me nervous. But still, as chaotic as the pets—specifically the dogs—can be, there's no denying the impact they can have on Grant when it comes to reining in his Asperger's. When Grant runs in the door after school each day, he goes immediately to check in with the dogs and the bird. When he's sad and no human can console him, he snuggles with a dog or two and suddenly he's pacified. I also saw this very clearly when we went to take our 2009 Christmas photos.

For many years, I had a hard time getting Grant to cooperate when we took family pictures, and it was nearly impossible to get a good one for the annual family Christmas card. Every year we knew that there would be a good chance we wouldn't get much time out of Grant for picture taking. When he was in the frame, he would be fidgeting and sliding all over the floor while we tried to hold him up and keep him still, let alone get him to smile and look at the camera. Thank goodness for modern technology—we were able to take Grant's image from other photos and swap them into new ones. Other people we know with Asperger's kids laugh when we talk about that because they know it all too well. One mother told me, "There have been years when we just left our son out of the picture. It wasn't worth the fight."

This year, though, I had pictures taken of the kids individually—each with a dog. Well, Grant was suddenly cooperative. With a dog in the frame, there was no problem. He was calm and rational, standing there in his Christmas sweater with a gigantic happy smile on his face and Rufus, the shar-pei/pug, at his side.

fourteen
Good-bye to All That

✳

FOR ALL THE PROGRESS THAT CURT AND I HAVE MADE WITH Grant, I'd be lying if I said there weren't still setbacks, and recently we've had to face a big one as we've come to realize that after the fourth grade, we might have to take Grant out of organized sports for good.

There's something about age eleven that makes parents and kids go a little bit bonkers when it comes to sports. Suddenly everyone starts taking games much more seriously at that age. During his sports seasons in 2009, Grant had a hard time keeping up with what was happening on the field, and we began to think it might not be safe for him. He and the other kids had finally reached sizes where some of Grant's foibles on the field—like just sitting there, in the middle of a game—could lead to him getting seriously hurt.

This has been a decision that we've really struggled with, and our minds are not made up. We haven't quite finished processing it ourselves. If and when we decide to take him out, we'll sit Grant down and explain our decision to him. I think we both feel that ultimately Grant needs to be the one making the decision, or at least it needs to seem that way. It's sad, because sports can help a kid like Grant learn to work with other people, and it's a good opportunity for socialization and making friends. Playing sports teaches kids good values. They learn how to be part of a team, and they learn sportsmanship. I know that for me, sports kept me doing well in school because if I didn't go to class, I couldn't play. I wanted to play, so I made it my business to do whatever was necessary to earn that right. Playing sports, you learn your limits, and how to reach past them, and how to recover from mistakes and move on.

As I'm sure you can imagine, with one member of the family being a professional athlete, sports are a big part of our life. It's strange to think of one of us being completely removed from participating in athletics, even though it might make sense. Even before I had a family, or even knew Curt, they were a big part of my life. I was raised watching just about every sport and playing field hockey, basketball, and softball. My mom played softball into her forties, with my dad coaching her. Sports played a part in nearly every conversation we had in our family. I even played my dad in a one-on-one basketball game for the chance to get my driver's license.

As a result of all this, sports were a cornerstone of the way I envisioned myself behaving as a parent. I saw myself as the perfect athlete-coach-mother. When we started our family, I assumed that sports would not just be Curt's job; they would be our life. I also assumed that being married to Curt, we'd produce at least a couple of serious athletes. I couldn't wait to coach them, and I thought that because of my interest in sports, I'd be able to coach all my kids at some level. With the other three, that has turned out to be the case. But with Grant, not so much.

Originally I'd suspected that Grant would be a natural athlete because he was big, and because he liked to run and throw his body into people (remember the failed Pop Warner football experiment). Simply in terms of build, he looked like he could be an athlete. But from an early age, way before Grant was diagnosed with Asperger's, I could never figure out how to engage him, at least not consistently. In his first year of soccer, he scored goal after goal—

until someone took the ball away from him just once, and then he refused to play offense. Some games he'd be on, but during others, I'd find him standing in the middle of the field, completely lost and disconnected from everything around him, almost as if he had forgotten he was in the game at all.

Meanwhile in basketball, there was too much running and too much going on for Grant to grasp it quickly enough, and football was dominated by instructions that needed far too much focus for someone as prone to spacing out as Grant.

In some respects, Grant's problem with baseball was just the opposite of his problems with basketball and football. Whereas basketball and football have too much frenetic energy, baseball has too little, which plays into Grant's tendency to be easily distracted. If Grant played in the outfield, there would be a good chance that he had no idea what was going on at the plate. And, of course, in baseball there's a completely unrealistic pressure applied to Grant because of his father that further complicates how he's treated by his teammates and coaches.

In the end, whatever sport he's playing, Grant spends a good bit of the time literally in his own world. Occasionally his coaches have to call time-outs because Grant has forgotten he's in a game at all and just zoned out. The coaches are afraid he'll get hurt, just standing there in the middle of the field. I don't blame them.

Just getting Grant to a practice or game has always been a challenge. Since Grant's diagnosis, my approach has changed, and there have been some good results. I've started informing him about a practice or a game a full day before, to begin prepping him for the change in routine. For a while it was still hard, really hard, to get him out the door, so I started telling him (again) about his practice or game hours before he needed to get dressed, allowing him time to stress out if need be, but also allowing me chances to get him into his uniform before his mood would change. Even with all this preparation, every game was an eight-hour ordeal.

Once we arrived at the field, it often became like many other things—he'd suddenly be fine. We'd remind him that he had to listen to the coaches and that it was not appropriate to take time-outs in my lounge chair on the opposite side of the playing field from his teammates. We'd also let him know what his teammates expected of him.

It helped that now Curt was there at Grant's games. He seemed to appreciate having his father there, and sometimes focused a little bit better with Curt present. But by the time they got home, Grant's mind was elsewhere. Grant doesn't think much about sports when he's not actually playing a game, as there's so much other stuff running around in that busy mind. Still, he's become more amenable to sports overall, and we've been able to enjoy watching him grow together.

Perhaps the most confusing thing for us as we tried to parent him through sports with Asperger's was that just as we thought he'd given up, every now and then he'd show interest in a particular aspect of a game. He would do this just often enough to make us think that he'd turned a corner. But it wouldn't last very long—often not even through a game, or half a game. It was the classic Asperger's focusing problem.

During his last soccer season in 2009, Grant talked the coach into letting him play goalie one day. I came very close to finding out the price of a new net, as Grant busied himself twisting his body in it, while his team was on offense. One time he got tangled up in the net and was unable to free himself in time to stop a goal. Never mind that everyone on the sidelines was yelling his name, *"Grant! Wake up, Grant!"* Afterward, he couldn't understand why his teammates had yelled at him. He thought they were being rude.

I never knew what I would get when I brought Grant to one of his practices or games. I never knew whether I would wind up proud or embarrassed. In one of his last soccer games, I felt a little of both. During that game, Grant's team was winning by a lot. I saw one of Grant's coaches call him over. He pointed and then positioned Grant in the direction of the goal. I knew what this meant: They were setting Grant up to take a shot.

For a second I could feel myself getting excited, thinking how great it was that they were giving him a chance to feel this. Grant went in and never moved from the spot where they told him to go. The ball came to him, and he shot and scored. All the parents on the sidelines cheered louder than I had heard them all season.

Grant immediately started jumping up and down. It was one of those special moments that just takes my breath away. For this incredible moment he was sharing in success at the same time as everyone around him. His happiness was in sync with everyone else's. It meant more than any goal, home run, touchdown, or basketball shot any of my kids had made before. It warmed my heart to the point that I wanted to cry, I was so proud and so happy for Grant. Everyone was happy for him. The whole team was shouting, *"Yay, Grant! Yay, Grant!"*

I was expecting the feel-good moment to continue when Grant came off the field. I ran over to him to give him a big hug, but he was unfazed and seemed to watch my enthusiasm with a sense of bemusement and distance.

"Grant," I said, "that was amazing! You did great."

Still, nothing. I couldn't believe it. Even though he'd jumped up and down at the moment he'd scored, now it somehow didn't matter. It was almost as if he'd forgotten he'd scored. It was puzzling, to say the least. I came down from my soccer goal high with an abrupt crash. I thought that for at least one bright and shining moment, Grant had wanted what every kid wanted—to score a goal—but I was wrong. He'd scored and he'd been excited, but it had been so fleeting. If I've learned one thing about being a sports parent it's that the fun of having your child score a goal isn't just the actual scoring, it's being able to share the moment with them and talk about it when they're off the field.

As it happened, I had brought Christina from YouthCare with me to that game. She had wanted to witness what happened with Grant around sports so that she could come up with strategies to help him.

"What do you make of his lack of excitement?" I asked her.

She didn't seem surprised at all. "Kids with Asperger's live only in the particular moment they're in," she explained. "The moment where he scored a goal, jumped up and down, and then high-fived his teammates has passed. All you can do is, the next game, remind him about the goal he scored and try to remind him of how good that felt. It might work and it might not work."

She also suggested videotaping his games. "It would give you a chance to share the moment with him and also to show him what is expected in that environment. Talk to him about the positive things he did in the game and what the effects of those were. Then refresh his memory before the next game and see if it keeps him on task and more focused."

This was one of those sobering moments when I realized once again that Grant really *is* different. He will always be different, whether or not he scores goals. Scoring is not going to be an indication that everything we've been going through with him is behind us. It never will be. For me, I now realize, that's the hardest lesson of all, the one that I resisted learning. Asperger's doesn't go away. This is who Grant is, and we need to accept him and love him, in all his quirky, emotional, adorable oddness.

I brought Grant to his game the next Saturday and did what Christina had recommended—reminding him of his goal in the prior game and how everyone was so proud of him for it. Even though Grant had quickly lost his enthusiasm about the goal he'd scored, I had high hopes that he'd engage again on the field. Maybe he'd connected with the sport in a new way that would keep him just a little more focused.

Except that didn't happen. For some reason, he just walked into the middle of the field, sat down, and started playing with the laces on his soccer shoes. He untied his shoes on the field in front of the team, and he didn't seem to care that the other kids would notice he didn't know how to retie them. He just focused on what made him comfortable, and at that moment what made him comfortable was playing with his shoelaces.

I sent Gehrig to go tell the coach to pull Grant, but before Gehrig even got there, they pulled him. Everyone was shouting, *"Grant! Grant! Grant!"*

I walked over toward the coaches. "We just took him out because we're afraid he's going to get hurt," one of them said.

"I know," I said. "I was going to tell you to take him out. I mean, if he's that despondent, there's no reason to have him in the game."

Here was a boy who'd scored a goal days before, and now he was sitting in the middle of field as if he had no idea that a game was going on. I had a lump in my throat. It may have been because we were coming up on Halloween, and he couldn't take his focus off of that. Who knew? With Grant, it could be anything.

I was baffled by it all. I still couldn't get over how quickly I went from that feeling of having my breath taken away and feeling so proud, to feeling confused and emotionally spent.

The icing on the cake: It was our turn to bring the popsicles for the team, and while everyone else played the game, Grant opened up the popsicles and played with them on the sidelines. When I got home, I felt completely wrung out. I had to sit down and regroup. I kept replaying the scenes of both games over and over in my mind. It hadn't sunken in with me yet—and it may never—that you can't apply logic to a lot of Grant's behavior. Even though I'd been learning about how randomly kids with Asperger's can behave from one minute to the next, for any number of reasons I still found myself trying to figure out what had gone wrong on that soccer field.

As I tried to digest how the scene had played out, I also found myself reviewing my behavior on the sidelines. Unusual as Grant's behavior was from one game to the next, what was truly difficult for me was not talking about his Asperger's to other parents. This was something I'd done a lot since his diagnosis, but I wish I hadn't. I'd found that I needed to explain why he didn't play like the other kids, though I knew full well that I was doing it for me, not for him. I knew that it only served to quell my own insecurities.

There was a difficult truth that I wasn't admitting to myself: I often felt embarrassed by Grant. That led to feeling ashamed and guilty about feeling embarrassed. So much of youth sports is about the community that you form with the other parents and kids on the team. As much as I'd improved in dealing with Grant in situations that involved other people, I was best with him in situations that involved total strangers. When it came to people who knew me or Curt, like parents at games, I was still struggling with what those people thought of me and my son. Through little fault of their own, other parents seemed to bring out the worst in my self-consciousness.

Still, there were some parents who would go for the jugular when it came to Grant's behavior on the field. Of course, it never helped anything to hear people who didn't even know Grant wonder why Curt Schilling's kid wasn't a better athlete.

"Why doesn't he know how to hold his glove?"

"Why isn't he a better batter?"

"Why doesn't he understand the rules?"

They weren't spending time with Grant. They knew nothing about him. So I'd tell them—partially to shut them up but more accurately to apologize for him. And that was something I needed to stop doing.

Of course, no one ever says or has said anything like that to Curt, at least not to his face. For his part, Curt cares very little about the level at which our kids perform on the athletic field. His only concerns are effort and ethics. He wants our children to play the games they play with honesty and integrity, but above all to have fun, no matter what they're doing. With Grant and sports, those are challenges, because some of his behavior can make it seem as if he is a "bad sport" or not hustling, which couldn't be further from the truth. Grant does what Grant *needs* to do at any given moment, and as someone who played professional sports for a living, witnessing that in Grant was Curt's biggest challenge.

After I'd replayed the whole apologizing-for-Grant scene in my head several times, I was all too aware that while Grant's behavior was appropriate to his Asperger's, mine was not. It was a hard realization to come to, but it was truly a wake-up call.

Since then, I've been better about not apologizing for Grant and letting him just be himself. It hasn't been easy, though, and I sometimes feel like I'm living in the last scene of the movie *Little Miss Sunshine*. In it, a little girl who is not classically pretty and not at all prepared enters a beauty pageant. Her grandfather helps her with the talent portion of the competition by teaching her to do a striptease. As she performs, the rest of her family is shocked, and everyone in the pageant's audience is appalled. In an attempt to make it seem as if there's nothing wrong or unusual with their young daughter's raunchy act, the parents jump up on stage with their daughter and dance. That's where I am now. I often feel like going out onto the field and doing a song-and-dance number to divert attention from Grant's antics.

Really, I never know what he's going to do next. Just recently, he was playing basketball and his team was throwing the ball in. He was behind his defender—and making rabbit ears. To whom, I have no idea. For two seconds, I cringed. Then I just started to laugh, and so did my mom.

I suppose my ability to laugh is a sign that I'm coming along. Even though he was operating on his own wavelength on the basketball court, as we left that day I realized that I was really proud of Grant for just going out there. And that's progress.

For all his struggles with sports, I have to give Grant credit for trying them. In his own way, he's given everything his best shot, even when he needed to be pushed headfirst into these things. They've certainly filled a different role in his life than I'd originally expected, but that doesn't mean they haven't been useful to his development, because they have.

Ultimately, his general ambivalence about sports makes it hard to predict how he'd feel about quitting, if that's what we decide he should do. There are some moments when he seems really interested in playing, but there are many more moments when he doesn't. If you ask him whether he wants to be signed up for soccer, he'll say yes, but then when you try to get him to leave the house for a soccer practice, after he screams *"Why did you sign me up for soccer?"*—well, good luck. Of course, that has a lot to do with his resistance to transitions, but once he's at the practice, he spends a good amount of time just spacing out.

What makes this a truly agonizing decision is that in the end it really is about safety. We'd be happy to let him continue to hang out at midfield and untie his shoelaces if we weren't concerned that his aloofness was a danger to him. Safety is a hard thing to compromise on, and no matter what Curt and I decide, that will undoubtedly be a big factor. We've come to find out that many children with Asperger's play individual sports like golf, swimming, and martial arts, and they excel because of their ability to focus so intently and obsessively on one thing. Maybe we'll focus more on his swimming, which he loves. Maybe that could be his thing. Maybe he'd be more consistently excited about that. We'll figure it out, I'm sure.

———•———

ONE OF THE REASONS I wanted Grant to play sports was that he didn't have many close connections, even at home. I had this idea that if he were a good athlete, he would find more common ground with all of us in the family and with other kids his age. I thought it would be one way for him to learn how to interact and get along with other kids, starting with his siblings. I figured sports was sort of a universal language—certainly the language of our family.

And I worry that with sports out of his life, it will distance him from his siblings even more. I wonder how he'll feel when he's the only one of our kids not playing. He definitely notices when there's excitement in the house about something one of the kids has done at a game—like when Gabby hit that grand slam. Will he feel left out of having chances to achieve things like that?

So far, though, playing sports hasn't given him too much to connect with his siblings on, and no amount of basketball, baseball, or soccer seems to help his ability to interact with them. He still barely notices when he's annoying them, and they have to put up with a lot. It's bad enough that I have to give in to Grant so often and let him choose the radio station we listen to, the DVD we watch, what we have for dinner. On top of that, Gehrig, Gabby, and Garrison have to deal with Grant's constant talking, and a lack of privacy when they have friends over.

Most kids don't want their little brothers around, no matter what they're like. Little brothers act like it's their job to bug older siblings and their friends. But it's not as if Gehrig and Gabby can just tell Grant to go away, because he won't. He doesn't realize he's doing anything wrong.

When the older kids have parties in our garage, we have to get Grant out of the house, because he walks into the garage and starts hanging out as if he's one of the gang. He'll just join the older kids and start talking. And talking. And talking. He repeats himself again and again. He listens to the older kids and picks up humor that's probably not even appropriate for them, and then repeats that humor ad nauseam. Sometimes he'll start fighting with Gehrig right in front of Gehrig's friends, and then hitting the friends to try to get them to play with him. Gehrig's friends are as patient as possible, but they also want their privacy when they're hanging out together. They're fourteen-year-old boys. They don't want to have to deal with a ten-year-old, especially one who has no sense of other people's boundaries.

Gabby goes out to other friends' houses a lot, but when she's at home with friends over, Grant decides it's a good idea to go and tell them stories that have no relevance to anything they might care about. He's oblivious to hints they make in an effort to get him to leave the room. He doesn't understand that his siblings might want to have some space for spending time with their friends—alone.

It's hardest on Garrison. He's Grant's constant playmate, and a very passive kid who idealizes both his big brothers. But like most kids, when Garrison has a friend over, he wants it to be *his* playdate. What I find is that when Garrison has a playdate at home, Grant takes it over, often making them do what he wants to do. The kid who is visiting doesn't know what to think, and sometimes feels bossed around by Grant.

The solution for me is usually to send Garrison out for playdates, or to schedule the ones at home when Grant isn't going to be there. On the flip side, when Grant has playdates at home, we need Garrison around in case Grant wanders away from his friend. Garrison is usually more than happy to pick up where Grant left off. But I wonder, how much longer will he be interested in that?

Here's the hardest lesson of all: How can you teach patience when you have none yourself? Not to mention that Grant is now at an age where social interaction is beginning to have a huge impact on how he feels about himself. We've often spoken with the older kids and tried to explain to them that Grant honestly doesn't intend to be mean, it's just his way of coping, his way of communicating, and Grant's way is and always will be different from ours. It's probably not realistic for us to expect kids of twelve and fourteen to "get it," since we're still trying to get it ourselves. They've definitely changed the way they interact with Grant, and they keep trying to improve in this area. But it remains a big challenge. Our greatest triumph in this area so far has been getting Gehrig and Gabby to come to us to help resolve a "Grant incident" rather than getting into a shouting match with him.

Grant's difficulty understanding how to have two-way interactions isn't limited to his siblings. There have begun to be some problems with kids outside our family. For instance, his friend had a birthday party recently. Grant had become obsessed with Chaotic cards and he got a starter pack for his friend as his birthday gift. But Grant insisted on bringing his own deck to the party, too. I tried to tell him that it wasn't a good idea.

"Grant, this isn't your party," I told him. "It's your friend's party. You need to let him have the attention and decide what games everyone is going to play." But Grant wouldn't listen to me.

Sure enough, it turned out to have been a bad idea. The birthday boy's friends made fun of Grant and his cards—apparently most of the ten-year-olds have outgrown them. But not Grant.

Even though the other kids were being mean, Grant didn't want to leave, because it was his friend's party. Still, he was hurt that the friend didn't stand up for him. Grant cried the whole way home. The part that confused me was that he wasn't crying because *he* had been made fun of. In his mind, at least, the problem was that they were making fun of the cards. It was almost as if the cards were Grant's babies, and someone was calling them ugly.

It was a classic Asperger's obsession with something, an attachment to his things that went far beyond that of our other kids to their toys. We try and take that into account when it comes to playing with others and sharing. To complicate things, he often switches obsessions unpredictably, at the drop of a hat. It makes for a very interesting Christmas each year. It's not out of the ordinary for Grant to assemble a Christmas wish list (replete with an appendix, a table of contents, and MapQuest directions to stores where said items can be purchased) and then a week later not want a single thing on the list. By then he will have found another passion, or another interest, leading to a completely new list.

When we returned from the party, Curt tried to talk to Grant, but he buried his head in the couch and flopped around, screaming into the cushions. We tried days later to talk to him about it, but he still refused—the wound was still too fresh. Eventually we hope to have a conversation with him about how he could have brought about a different outcome. We'll want to help him try to understand why taking the cards wasn't such a good idea after all.

Still, as problematic as Grant's obsession with Chaotic cards proved to be in this case, I have faith that some of his interests will eventually lead him to find like-minded friends. There are plenty of kids who don't have Asperger's who still get focused on things that are no longer "age appropriate." I can only hope that some of the work we're doing with Grant will help him to meet kids who are into similar things, so that when he comes into contact with them, he'll be able to spot a kindred spirit. In the meantime, I try to tell myself that being a nerd isn't the end of the world. I mean, look at Curt. He turned out all right.

fifteen
Lessons for a Mother from a Son

✳

IMAGINE YOU'RE IN THE MIDDLE OF GIVING A PRESENTATION to a huge audience of all the most important people at your job, and your mind suddenly goes blank. You know you're supposed to say something, that the crowd in the room is waiting for you to say something, but for one reason or another you just can't muster the words that are expected of you. You look down at your notes, at your PowerPoint slide. You search the room, trying to read the faces of the people around you, but they all hold the same vacant, emotionless stare. Your mental processes go on total anxiety overload. Your thoughts and feelings become nearly impossible to distinguish and blend together into one seemingly inseparable reaction that's impossible to contain.

This is what kids with Asperger's feel like every day, in every situation that comes up that they are not prepared for. This is why they like schedules and routines. It's comforting for them to have details they can count on when they feel otherwise out of control. Schedules and routines help them feel prepared. They like things to perfectly match their expectations, and have a very difficult time dealing with any variation on what they thought was coming.

But life doesn't come with an activity schedule, and this more than anything else is what preparing for a future with Grant is all about. Probably the most difficult aspect of Grant's Asperger's is accepting the permanence of it. That, and the guilt I bear about having missed the clues for so long and treated him harshly under the assumption that he was simply disrespectful of me. I will probably wrestle with that for the rest of my life. I don't know if I'll ever forgive myself.

But as hard as it has been to come to terms with the past, what I've come to realize is that we are only at the beginning of understanding Asperger's, and it's going to take many years of trying things to figure out how to help Grant cope and succeed. There will most likely be a good deal of trial and error, since there are still many things unknown about Asperger's, plus ever-evolving and conflicting schools of thought. One set of doctors would insist that we cut certain foods from his diet and prescribe homeopathic remedies. Another would prescribe various pharmaceuticals. On the advice of other parents who have tried diet change with no great results, we've decided to spare ourselves the added drama of trying to wean Grant off the many common foods that contain wheat and dairy. We're of the mind that there's no wonder drug for Asperger's, although Grant does take Adderall, which helps a ton with his ADHD.

There is no one-size-fits-all solution. One of Grant's teachers recently said to me, "If you've met one kid with Asperger's, you've only met one." Some characteristics are consistent from one Asperger's kid to another, but each case is unique. Whether with sports or animals, transferring schoolwork to the computer or breaking his homework into smaller chunks, we'll have to keep finding what works for Grant in particular.

While learning what's behind Grant's unusual behavior has been helpful and has taught us how *not* to react to him, it's still often a mystery knowing how *to* react. And often the techniques that work with him on most days just don't work on others. That's the thing about Asperger's, you never know what you're going to get. We keep our fingers crossed with each interaction with Grant, hoping it goes smoothly. But every single one has the potential to turn into a disagreement.

A couple of recent flare-ups took me by surprise. The first happened at the dentist's office. The last time we went, Grant was perfectly charming and obedient, which was not the norm. Like most kids, Grant was never particularly fond of the chair or the dentist, and his Asperger's makes it extremely difficult for him to get through an appointment. After that last appointment, I thought maybe we had come to a new place with him and dentistry. But this time he was completely out of control. The dentist couldn't even get him to open his mouth so she could count his teeth. He'd open it long enough to scream, and then shut it. And he flipflopped in the chair.

It wasn't until the dentist negotiated with him to choose a flavor of toothpaste and brush his own teeth that he came around. Maybe it was because she gave him something he could do on his terms—choose a flavor, and brush his own teeth. Still, I didn't see that one coming. And by the time he mellowed out, I thought I was going to lose it.

The second incident was dinner at IHOP. I went there with the three boys on a night when Gabby and Curt had other obligations. The kids all love pancakes, and there are many other things on the menu, too, which makes it an easy option for Grant, who is always so difficult to please at dinner. You never know what foods he's into refusing and which he's stuck on, hoping to eat them every night, as on his recent steak streak. Taking him to a place where he'd have choices seemed to eliminate one problem for the evening. I thought it was a no-brainer; no matter what he was into, it was probably on the IHOP menu.

For some reason, though, Grant decided on the drive that he didn't want to go to dinner there. Just like that, even though I had prepared him by telling him the plan earlier, and he seemed fine with it. Even though I now know this is a characteristic of kids with Asperger's, it still amazes me how rigid Grant can be. I have to remind myself that it's not because he wants to be a pain in the neck. It's because of his processing issues and his neurological inclination toward emotional overload. "I'm not eating there," Grant said. I just continued to drive. He said it over and over again. When we pulled up to the restaurant, I said, "Okay, out of the car."

"*No!*" he insisted.

So I took Gehrig and Garrison in. We were parked in view of the front door, so I could watch him from inside. After about fifteen minutes, Grant came in and was fuming. "*You left me in the car!*" he yelled, and then refused to sit with us. He sat at a table across the aisle instead.

"Would you like something to eat?" I asked, trying to neutralize the situation. In the past I would have scolded him, but instead I just let him sit there, knowing that harsh words would only escalate the problem and further ruin Grant's appetite. At that point I figured that during the extra time in the car he might have gotten hungry and/or sorted out his feelings. But apparently not.

"*No!*" he yelled. "*I'm not eating!*"

I quietly asked the waitress to bring him some pancakes anyway. In the past it's been hard for him to resist eating when everyone around him was, although that has never kept him from yelling at me when the food arrived, anyway—even when he has gone ahead and eaten it. But that stage was apparently over, because that night he still wasn't willing to touch his food. "*I told you I'm not eating it!*" he yelled.

I told the waitress to just put it down, and when she did, Grant pushed it to the other side of the table. *Great,* I thought. *Now he's made the waitress feel uncomfortable.*

I didn't know what to do with myself. Just then, Gehrig looked at me. "Mom," he asked, "how do you do this every day?"

I was touched by Gehrig's recognizing my struggle, and for a moment, felt less alone. "Deep breaths," I answered.

When we got home that night, sure enough, Grant asked me for something to eat.

"Okay," I said, "but you're going to have to make it yourself, buddy." That was it—once again he was set off.

"I told you I wasn't willing to eat there and you made me go!" he shouted, completely unaware of the fact that there were three other people who were perfectly willing to eat at IHOP. In other homes, when the mom says, "We're going to dinner there and that's it," *that's it.* But not in our house, not with Grant. Sometimes there's just no way for me to win.

As frustrating as confrontations like these can be, one of the more helpful side effects of Grant getting older is that he's beginning to have more self-awareness (sometimes) about his behavior and realize that his actions have an impact on the other people around him. Occasionally he'll come to me a few hours or even days after one of his blow-ups, once he's had some time to process everything.

"Mom," he'll ask sheepishly, "are you mad?"

That gives us a chance to talk about the situation on his terms, which would never work in the heat of the moment. When a kid with Asperger's is lost in his emotions, you don't stand a chance of helping him understand what's going on and what's wrong with his behavior. When you go back later and revisit the situation, you have an opportunity to talk about other choices they might make the next time. In those instances, I can resolve things with Grant—but not without getting completely drained. Still, the mere fact that we're able to have those conversations is encouraging, and a perfect example of something that we wouldn't have been able to do even a year ago.

———◆———

WHILE GRANT'S ASPERGER'S CAN be exasperating, there are aspects of it that lead to moments of great laughter, too. Perhaps the best part of growing more comfortable with it is that I feel as if for the first time in a long time I'm able to loosen up and laugh.

One of his funnier characteristics is his penchant for blurting out painfully honest statements. If Grant has a thought or a feeling, he can't hold it in. It's one of the reasons he and so many other kids with Asperger's have difficulty in social situations. They say the things that other people just think but keep to themselves for fear of hurting someone's feelings.

For example, there's a woman who comes to clean our house on Thursdays. She has a lot of stories to tell, and she likes to talk. *A lot.* One day, when she was there and chatting, Grant went right up to her and said, "Man, do you ever stop talking?" I tried hard not to laugh. It was especially funny to me because it was exactly what I had been thinking.

Curt has fallen victim to Grant's blurting, too. Curt has a tendency to rush through meals, eating very quickly. One time when we were in Puerto Rico, we went to a Japanese restaurant where they had a hibachi. They cook your food right in front of you and serve many courses, cooking the whole time. Well, by the time the food was on the table, Curt was practically done with his portion. We all noticed it, but only Grant said anything about it.

"You've gotta slow down, Dad," he said. "What's your hurry?"

At school, Grant recently learned that chewing tobacco is a drug. Curt unfortunately chews it, and one day, when the two of them were together, Curt stopped at a convenience store to get some. Well, when Grant heard Curt ask for the tobacco, he became very vocal.

"I can't believe this place sells you drugs?!" he shouted at the top of his lungs, over and over again. Curt kept trying to quiet him, but he wouldn't stop.

It's hard not to get mad at him in moments like that. It can seem as if he's being disrespectful. But like me, Curt is coming to accept that Grant says those things simply because he doesn't have the same mental filters we have. When he says things like that, we try to guide him by telling him, "That's not a very nice thing to say." In the moment, we both attempt to keep a straight face so that he knows we're serious. But when Grant isn't around, we laugh out loud every time we retell the stories.

Maybe it's funnier when he's brutally honest with other people, though. Not long ago, I went bathing suit shopping. We were going on vacation. I hadn't worn a bathing suit in years—not since I'd had melanoma.

Grant was with me at the store. I grabbed a few suits and tried one on. When I came out of the dressing room to look at myself in the mirror, I asked Grant, "So, what do you think?"

"Well," he said, "You look like a forty-year-old trying to look fifty." My jaw dropped.

"What did you just say?" I asked, shocked and insulted. Then I composed myself. "Did you mean that I looked like a forty-year-old who was trying to look thirty?"

"No," he said. "You look like you're trying to look fifty." Well, I guess that was his honest opinion. He didn't mean to hurt my feelings. But you can be sure I skipped the bikinis and went right for the one-piece suits.

It's not all Don Rickles humor, though. Grant's incredible sweetness can also be a source of some very funny and touching moments—like the note that I got from his fourth-grade teacher, Miss Hayes.

"Grant made me chuckle when he figured out I was a 'Miss,'" she wrote. "He was very concerned for me that I don't have a husband. It was genuinely very innocent and cute. I should have him talk to my mom about it. Together they could worry."

When Grant was in the third grade he kept pestering Mrs. Trikulous to let him read a story he had written. She kept putting him off, telling him it was not the time for his story to be read, not to mention that the story he'd written was something he'd done of his own volition—it hadn't been a classroom assignment. But he kept on and on until finally she relented and let him read his story. She was quickly bowled over by the story he'd written. He'd made every kid in the class a heroic character in a fantasy tale. And he'd done it all for the sake of making his classmates smile, which he did.

Around that time, Grant told me that when he grew up, he wanted to be a policeman so he could always protect me. That melted my heart.

This sweetness and sensitivity toward others is something that I don't think Grant will outgrow. It seems to be a part of who he is—Asperger's or not. He likes to know that people he loves are taken care of, and he's as attuned as ever to people who are in need. We now know that's the reason Grant gravitates toward kids who have special needs, like William and Stephen. Stephen is Grant's best friend these days. From one year to the next, the school keeps Stephen and Grant in the same class. Stephen has a special aide in class with him, and the aide keeps an eye on Grant, too.

Grant sometimes takes it upon himself to help Stephen out. One day, as school was ending, the aide told Stephen it was time to get up from circle time and go. Stephen either didn't hear her or didn't want to leave. After she'd said it a few times, Grant went over to Stephen and said, "Stephen, go get your bag. Go get your bag, then come back over and sit down. She has told you twice."

The teacher, holding back her laughter, interrupted. "It's okay, Grant," she said. "I've got it."

"No, I beg to differ," Grant told the teacher in all seriousness. "He didn't move until I told him to."

It's inspiring to witness Grant's friendship with Stephen. It has had a positive effect on both of them. Grant gets to be very responsible, always keeping an eye out for his friend, and Stephen learns how to be more of a typical little boy. He emulates Grant—which can be both a good thing and a bad thing. Stephen learned to pee standing up from Grant, which might not seem like rocket science, but it is something that helps him feel more like everyone else.

Though Grant does very well in friendships with special needs kids like William and Stephen, he continues to have a harder time with kids who are considered "normal," and this remains a huge source of anxiety for me. As he gets older, this inability will become more and more of an issue, because Grant's maturity in certain areas will be delayed. He is ahead of his years in terms of empathy and emotional insight, but he is very young in other ways.

Last year in third grade, he was into writing short stories in school. It was amazing, because he let his imagination fly and came up with some really great stories about castles and kings. At recess, he'd try to bring his stories to life outside. He'd say, "Okay, guys, so this is the castle," and he'd point to something on the playground. He'd make a big elaborate plan, and the kids would wait for him to tell them what to do. Then they'd all play out the story that Grant had made up.

But in fourth grade, kids are not as into imagination games—although Grant still is. Now they don't want to play like that. I feel sad that it's becoming something that isn't appropriate for him, because he really loves using his mind in that way. The larger concern is that he'll still want to play like that as he gets older, and as a result he'll further isolate himself socially. We don't know, and no one can tell us for sure, when he'll "catch up" socially. When he's twenty-five, it won't so much matter, but at eight, ten, and twelve, those differences can be enormous.

At the moment, though, these concerns are only in my mind. They make for one of the hardest parts of being Grant's mom, though I am pleased to report that he was recently the star of the week at his school, which meant that each child had to write him a note. Almost all the kids wrote, "You are always nice to me." It filled my heart!

At least for now, Grant doesn't seem to care whether other kids think he's cool, which is incredibly refreshing for a person like me who has spent far too much of her life being preoccupied with what other people think. Grant marches to the beat of his own drummer (and by the way, he has recently taken to playing the drums—a passion nurtured by my dad's recent purchase

of the loudest set of drums on earth for him), regardless of the social consequences. This became especially obvious this year when he went to the fourth
grade dance—his first dance ever.

I prepared him way in advance. All week I kept telling him, "You know
what this Friday is, right? After drums and soccer practice, you have the
fourth grade dance."

He was so excited about the dance that he couldn't eat. We were having
ham slices and potatoes that night, and he loves those, but he just sat there in
a daze, unable to put food in his mouth.

Curt said, "You are not going to the dance unless you eat," and Grant was
caught because he really wanted to go to the dance, but he was also too anxious to be able to eat. We negotiated with him and settled on a biscuit.

After dinner, he went upstairs to get ready. He'd already picked out his
clothes—he knew just what he wanted to wear, which I thought was cute.
After he changed, he came downstairs and said, "Mom, I have to talk to
you."

Uh-oh. I couldn't imagine what it was going to be about. A girl maybe?
There was one he had his eye on. He really loved her and had for years. If
Grant's not in nerd mode, he has the potential to be a real lady's man.

"I want to wear real sneakers, Mom," he said. "I want to wear sneakers
that tie."

"Okay," I said. Except he didn't own any sneakers with laces. Because he
can't tie his shoelaces, we've never bought a pair of shoes with laces that aren't
soccer cleats. I'd long ago stopped worrying about the fashion statement of
Velcro, but in this instance we were stuck. The best I could do was to grab a
pair of Gabby's basketball sneakers that fortunately didn't look like girls'
shoes, but they were still too big for him. They were a size seven, and he is
only a size four. However, he actually liked that because it meant he could slip
in and out of them if he needed to, without having to retie anything.

We went over shoelace tying for a few minutes. After several tries, I couldn't believe it: He actually did it! There are some moments in your child's life that you just know you'll remember, not because they're the most important, but because they feel that way. This was one of those moments for me.

I smiled at him as he ran out of the car to the dance that night. I didn't care that Grant was wearing Gabby's shoes, or that they were too big. I didn't worry about whether he would embarrass himself, or whether other kids would make fun of his shoes, whether the teachers would judge me or whether other parents would wonder why I let him out of the house that night. All I cared about was that for the first time Grant had tied his shoes on his own.

Grant went to the dance and had a great time. He texted me from the dance and informed me: "I am never coming home." I laughed and heaved a sigh of relief. When I went to pick him up afterward, he came bolting out.

The next Monday, when Christina came to work with us, we talked about the shoes. All night, at the dance, kids told Grant that his shoes were too big. But that didn't seem to bother him at all.

"Grant doesn't realize that other people might have different thoughts or opinions than he does on any given subject," Christina said.

In his opinion, the shoes were perfect because they were lace-ups. That was all that mattered to him about them, and so that was all that mattered to me.

There's no denying that I admire Grant for not paying other people's opinions too much mind. It's the opposite of what I have always done. In fact, I have let other people's opinions keep me from doing things I really wanted and needed to do. Grant, though, wore the big shoes to the dance and was very proud of himself. Frequently I find myself thinking back to the time the girls in junior high made fun of me for wearing pants that were too short, and I'd spent the whole day hiding in the bathroom. I'd been "normal," and there was nothing that could have protected me from those girls trying to make me feel "different." Grant, on the other hand, is comfortable with himself. Nothing and no one can change that.

————•————

IT'S AMAZING HOW MUCH this experience with Grant has changed me. It has opened my eyes and my heart, it has loosened me up, it has shifted my priorities, and it is beginning to help me stop caring so much about what other people think of me.

As strange as it may sound, in every area of my life there are ways in which I have actually benefited from having a child with Asperger's. I have become more patient with all the kids I encounter, not just at home but on the teams I coach. I'm taking sports less seriously, and that is making me a better coach. I have coached Gabby's softball and basketball teams since she started playing, and I will admit that when I started coaching her in softball, I took it much more seriously than I should have or than she did. I was always a fun coach, but I was too serious about her doing well.

I remember that when Gabby was eight, she preferred to get hit with the softball rather than swing. Sometimes she'd let herself get struck out, never taking the bat off her shoulder. Once, after she did that, she came back to the dugout and I said, through gritted teeth, "If you strike out again and don't take that bat off your shoulder, I am going to be so mad!"

Gabby looked me right in the eye. "Softball is fun, Mom," she said, "and you're taking the fun right out of it." She was right, but it's taken Grant to make me realize just how right she was.

Dealing with Grant has forced me to hold a mirror up to myself, and the view hasn't always been flattering. It's uncomfortable to admit this, but I realize now that before his diagnosis, I really didn't like myself. I mean, I wasn't a bad person and my heart was certainly in the right place when it came to my husband, our family, and the people around us, but I always worried too much about how I appeared to everyone watching our life from the sidelines. I was vain, rigid, and uptight. That drew me away from experiencing and appreciating the pure joy that life can bring.

Now I'm no longer afraid of a life I can't predict or plan out. My kids can wear pajamas to the movies, costumes to the grocery store, or girls' basketball shoes to a dance. Let people talk. What does it really matter? If I make them good kids who respect people, who cares what they're wearing?

Grant doesn't care what other people think—to a fault. That frees him up to live more genuinely. When Grant laughs, it's an infectious laugh. When he cries, it's out of genuine sadness. And when he loves, it's without stipulations or fear. It's true and deep. When he's difficult, it's not out of malice or disrespect. It's simply a matter of his neurological inability to process certain kinds of information and a need for specific types of physical stimulation. And while my fears about Grant's social awkwardness keep me up at night, I realize that there's a lot I can learn from Grant about being true to my own opinions and needs.

Grant made me accountable in ways I hadn't yet been. He forced me to face and understand people and things that used to leave me terribly uncomfortable. While having a child with Asperger's is certainly a challenge, I realize that there will always be parents who are facing much greater tragedies. I spent all of Curt's career meeting families who had lost loved ones and hearing the cries of parents of very sick children. Grant is healthy. All my kids are healthy. And now that I have this new perspective, I feel especially fortunate.

I have stopped comparing my kids to others the way society pressures you to. Now I celebrate my kids' differences and the qualities that make them unique and special, rather than obsessing over ways in which they need to improve. Instead of waiting for my kids to do something that makes me feel as if I'm succeeding as a parent, I just have faith that I am. I hardly ever get mad at the kids anymore. I realize life is too short, and there are too many good things you might miss about your kids if you're always fighting with them.

I have become more compassionate toward others. I no longer judge when I come across people in sour moods, or parents having a hard time controlling their kids. I have been those persons at their wits' end, I have been that parent, and I have that child.

No one has taught me more effectively than Grant that I can't control everything in my world. After living in fear for so long about what might go wrong each day, now I wake up every morning excited about what the day may bring—good or bad. I've become more patient, and I've slowed down. I used to be so busy hurrying to the next stage in life that I never enjoyed the one I was in. Now, when I think that in eleven years I will no longer have kids at home, I get scared, and sad.

Above all, I realize now more than ever that I am a lucky woman. I have a beautiful family with four unique, happy kids, and a great—rejuvenated— marriage with my loving husband. Our year spent in therapy with Dr. Xavier proved to be a decision that may very well have saved our marriage. We learned how to talk and listen to each other. We remembered why we fell in love with each other in the first place. Therapy together was the best thing we could have done, for ourselves and our kids. I never imagined that I'd be more in love with my husband seventeen years into our marriage than when we first met, but I am.

Now I'm more happily married than I have ever been. There is so much love in the house that sometimes our kids are actually grossed out by it. We are friends again and now parents together. If people wonder why Curt retired from baseball and doesn't miss it, just think about the last year of our lives and that's pretty much the answer.

Grant and Curt continue to work things out. It's not without its challenges, but the fact that they both have ADHD, and both have what I consider "nerd hobbies" means that their next intersection of common ground isn't far off. Curt's always played games that the boys go in and out of enjoying, so even though sports doesn't appear to be on Grant's future schedule, they'll keep finding things to do together.

I'm not sure how I got here, but I'm smiling, and I'm writing—something I couldn't do just two years ago, when I first received Grant's diagnosis. As with any events in our lives that shake us up, it has taken me time to heal and to grieve over what I felt I lost. But having done that, I'm ready to get on a new path. It took a long time to reach this particular point, where I can be open about what's going on with Grant—with myself and with others. It's a journey that has only just begun.

I have never asked why this happened to us, although sometimes I wonder whether it wasn't for a positive reason. Many people wonder why, if there is a God, we have grief and sadness in the world. It seems simple to me: Without those things, we can't truly celebrate what brings us joy. You need shadow to appreciate light. When people say, "God never gives you more than you can handle," I laugh and reply, "I'm asking him for a little break."

Even though life has thrown me many curveballs over the past ten years, I truly do understand how blessed I am. I thank God for all that I have. Grant may keep me on an emotional roller coaster where I feel proud one minute, sad the next, and uplifted the one after that. No matter. I still thank God every day that he gave Grant to me. He has truly been a gift in my life.

That's not to say that everything is all better; I still struggle with grief around Grant's issues. On the one hand, it's great that he gets to live truthfully, and never has to concern himself with conforming or playing mind games. He's just not capable of that, and I think it's beautiful. He is a most loving, compassionate creature, and I believe he will find people who appreciate those qualities in him.

On the other hand, when he moves into adolescence, it will probably be very hard on Curt and me—much harder than it will be on Grant. We can see him differently than he sees himself; we can notice that he is different from the other kids. Grant can't see that, and who knows? Maybe ignorance is bliss.

The more I learn about Grant's Asperger's, the more I adore him. He is a source of pure, unconditional love. He makes me laugh, he makes me cry. He sometimes makes me want to scream. But he also makes me more compassionate. Although I can't always comfort him and get him to behave on my terms, when he hugs me, I know it is genuine, that it is exactly what he wants to be doing. He has no other motive than to express his love for me. Words can't describe how good that feels to a mother.

appendix
Asperger's Resources

As I learned by being a parent of a child with Asperger's syndrome, it's easier to handle when you have help from other people and you're armed with ample information. Here are some of the books and organizations that have helped me along the way. I hope they will help you, too. Remember, you are not alone. Best wishes on your journey.

BOOKS ABOUT ASPERGER'S

Asperger's Association of New England. *An Introduction to Asperger Syndrome: Information for Families of Children and Adolescents.* Watertown, MA: Asperger's Association of New England, October 2006.

Attwood, Tony. *Asperger's Syndrome: A Guide for Parents and Professionals.* Philadelphia: Jessica Kingsley Publishers, January 1998.

———. *The Complete Guide to Asperger's Syndrome.* Philadelphia: Jessica Kingsley Publishers, May 2008.

Baker, Linda J., and Lawrence A. Welkowitz. *Asperger's Syndrome: Intervening in Schools, Clinics, and Communities.* Mahwah, NJ: Lawrence Erlbaum Associates, July, 2004.

Barnhill, Gena. *Right Address, Wrong Planet: Children with Asperger Syndrome Becoming Adults.* Shawnee Mission, KS: Autism Asperger Publishing, February 2002.

Bolick, Teresa. *Asperger Syndrome and Adolescence: Helping Preteens and Teens Get Ready for the Real World.* Beverly: MA: Fair Winds Press, June 2004.

———. *Asperger Syndrome and Young Children: Building Skills for the Real World.* Beverly, MA: Fair Winds Press, July 2004.

Buron, Kari Dunn, and Mitzi Curtis. *The Incredible 5 Point Scale: Assisting Students with Autism Spectrum Disorders in Understanding Social Interactions and Controlling Their Emotional Responses.* Shawnee Mission, KS: Autism Asperger Publishing, January 2004.

Koris, Ellen. *Asperger Syndrome: An Owner's Manual—What You, Your Parents, and Your Teachers Need to Know: An Interactive Guide and Workbook.* Shawnee Mission, KS: Autism Asperger Publishing, March 2006.

Myles, Brenda Smith, and Jack Southwick. *Asperger Syndrome and Difficult Moments: Practical Solutions for Tantrums, Rage and Meltdowns.* Shawnee Mission, KS: Autism Asperger Publishing, March 2005.

Welton, Jude. *Can I Tell You About Asperger Syndrome? A Guide for Family and Friends.* Philadelphia: Jessica Kingsley Publishers, January 2004.

MEMOIRS

Page, Tim. *Parallel Play: Growing Up with Undiagnosed Asperger's.* New York: Doubleday, September 2009.

Paradiz, Valerie. *Elijah's Cup: A Family's Journey into the Community and Culture of High-Functioning Autism and Asperger's Syndrome.* Philadelphia: Jessica Kingsley Publishers, March 1996.

Robison, John Elder. *Look Me in the Eye: My Life with Asperger's.* New York: Crown, September 2007.

MOVIE

Adam. Directed by Max Mayer. 2009, in which Adam, a lonely man with Asperger's syndrome, develops a relationship with his upstairs neighbor, Beth.

ORGANIZATIONS

Asperger's Association of New England

85 Main Street, Suite 101

Watertown, MA 02472

Phone: (617) 393-3824

http://www.aane.org/

Best Buddies

100 Southeast Second Street, Suite 2200

Miami, FL 33131

Toll Free: (800) 89 BUDDY (892-8339)

http://www.bestbuddies.org/

U.S. Autism and Asperger Association

P.O. Box 532

Draper, UT 84020-0532

Phone: (801) 816-1234

http://www.usautism.org/

YouthCare Camp

Massachusetts General Hospital

15 Green Street, Third Floor

Charlestown, MA 02129

Phone: (617) 726-0060

Fax: (617) 726-0064

http://www2.massgeneral.org/youthcare/

Acknowledgments

There are many people without whom this book would not have been possible, and I extend my gratitude to them all.

To Sari Botton, for listening to my stories for hours, and with your special gift of writing, helping me to dig deep into myself to do something I never dreamed I could. Without our relationship, these words would never have made it to paper. Thank you for the crash course.

To Matt Harper, my editor, for your encouragement and words of kindness to make me believe I could do this. But above all, thanks for your special talent in editing, helping to make sure the focus was kept on Grant, and what I felt so strongly about from the beginning.

To Lisa Sharkey, for taking a chance on me based on a speech, and believing that this story would help many other people.

I thank you, Katie Leighton. Without you, this book would never have happened. You insisted that this was something important for me to do when I didn't yet understand it myself. Thank you for your friendship!

To Dr. Peter Rosenberger, our neurologist, thank you for the compassion you showed when helping me understand Grant, and for always helping me believe it would all be okay when I couldn't see the light at the end of the tunnel.

To Dr. Maura Shaunessy, our family physician, thank you for treating me as a friend and guiding me with such care to the next step in healing, but not before I was ready. You gave me the push I needed, at just the right time.

To Dr. Jesine Xavier, thank you for not seeing us as anything but a couple in love and showing us how to see that in ourselves. Our family has been forever changed by that.

To Dr. Jan Weathers, for helping me pull down the guard I hid behind for so many years so I could learn to laugh at and love all that life brings me—the good and the bad.

To Pastor Phil Bauman, thank you always for your teachings, which inspire me to be the best person I can.

To Mrs. Callahan, Mrs. Trikulous, Miss Hayes, and all the teachers and educators who have worked with Grant over the years, your patience and true love of teaching will forever have an impact on Grant and my family. Thank you for always seeing that Grant has so much love, and never hesitating to tell us what happiness he brought to your classroom, and to you.

To the Asperger's Association of New England, thanks for the knowledge and resources you offer to families. I hope that more people will realize how important and invaluable your organization was to us and can be to them.

To Brenda Dater, Katy Stromland, and Christine Connelly, thank you for treating me like a regular mom who needed help. You made me feel like I wasn't alone, and as if I could really do this. I hope I can do for others what you did for me. You were my first steps toward peace of mind.

To YouthCare, I am so proud that Grant can be a part of this wonderful camp. I hope that through my sharing of this story, others in your field will be inspired to start similar programs elsewhere. To all of those counselors, I applaud your time and hard work, and hope you realize how your patience and love changes each family like ours.

To YouthCare director Scott McLeod, Ph.D., thank you for always having the time not just for our family but all families you come into contact with who need your help. Your passion to make this an easier world for kids like Grant will change their lives.

To YouthCare counselor Christina Lazdowsky, I often laugh when I am reminded that you are twenty years younger then I am. Your wealth of knowledge, which you so generously share with me, changes our home and gives us hope that we are doing everything possible to get Grant ready to go out on his own and face the world.

To Marilyn Davis, thank you for being that extra set of hands. You have personally had two very rough years, losing two daughters, and yet you are always there for us. Thank you for telling me I "got it" when I was writing this book. Nice to know I never have to worry when you're around. You are a treasure.

To the Medfield community, thank you for giving us the privacy and respect we needed in order to put our roots down and make this our home.

To all the coaches and volunteers in and out of the classroom, thank you for giving back. You do not get enough recognition. Know that you are appreciated.

To my friends Heidi, Jen, Linda, Ellen, Peg, Lisa J., Robyn, Lisa M., Reka, and Janet, thank you for all the hugs and check-ins to make sure I was okay, and the endless tears of joy and sadness that we shared over the years—plus the ones yet to come. Where would I be without my girlfriends?

To Sue Gorham, who runs SHADE, and Ellyn Phillips, of the Philadelphia chapter of the ALS Association, thank you both for showing me how to make a real difference in people's lives, not just by raising money, but also by touching each life with friendship. You taught me that you change the world not alone, but by touching one life at a time. Thank you to all the people at SHADE and the ALS Association for all your hard work for these most important causes that are so close to my heart. And to the good people at Families of SMA, who do so much for children like Grant's friend William.

To my brother Michael, my sisters-in-law, Allison and Shelby, my brother-in-law, Larry, Aunt B., Uncle Billy, and Pam, thank you for swooping in with kind words and/or visits when you could sense I was starting to fall apart. I love you all.

Mom and Dad, thank you for the foundation you gave me growing up, helping me to become a good person. You led by example and always loved me unconditionally. By the way, you always said I would get paid back when I had kids. I did. Thank you for believing in me when I didn't always think it was possible to achieve the things I wanted. You taught me always to fight for what I believed was right. And look at that—you couldn't get me to read a book when I was growing up, and now I wrote one! I hope if nothing else, I made you proud. I love you both very much even if I don't tell you enough.

I can't thank you enough, Curt, for giving me these beautiful kids. You have always made me feel like no one in the world could love me any more than you do. Your passion for life is contagious. You have always stood by your word from the beginning that no matter how hard things got, you weren't going anywhere. Your love makes me feel safe. I love you and thank you for encouraging me on this project, and for the hours you devoted to going over final drafts, toward the end. How about this book? It's a long way from spell-checking my grocery list. By the way, it's official: I am funnier. It is now written in a book. I love you, Curt.

To my kids: You are the reason I get up every morning. You make me want to love more deeply than I ever knew I could. Gehrig, Gabby, and Garrison, you are each wonderful human beings who make me smile with pride every day. Being your mom is all I have ever wanted to be. I love you very much.

And to Grant, thank you for letting me share our story with the world. I wish sometimes that I could be more like you. You love life and you don't live it the way anyone else expects you to. You are free to be exactly what you want to be. You will do amazing things in life, and I can't wait to see what they are. I love you, Bug!